"Leadership has become a critical aspect of not only professional development, but human development, which is why mindfulness has become fundamental to leadership's ability to make a meaningful, sustainable impact in business. *Mindfulness and Business Education* will no doubt become an invaluable resource for business leaders seeking to unlock a deeper sense of motivation, inspiration, and connection with not only their work, but themselves."

Anita Mendiratta, *Special Advisor to the Secretary General – UN Tourism*

"Essential reading for anyone who would like to know how to bring mindfulness practices into management learning and education, build 'awareness intelligence', and unlock untapped potential in the next generation of self-aware and responsible leaders and managers."

Eugene Sadler-Smith, *Professor of Organizational Behaviour, University of Surrey, UK*

MINDFULNESS AND BUSINESS EDUCATION

Mindfulness and Business Education: Developing self-aware future leaders is a practical guide for educators and academics with teaching responsibilities in business schools or colleges. Business schools have a responsibility to equip future leaders with the right knowledge and the right skills to make the right decisions, particularly in times of volatility, uncertainty, complexity, and ambiguity. This responsibility can only be met if business schools change the way they teach and develop self-aware future leaders who are grounded in the foundations of mindfulness.

The book is divided into three parts: Why, What, and How. Part One: Why introduces the foundations of mindfulness, draws on the history of business school development, and discusses leadership approaches presently taught in business schools. Part Two: What discusses ways of measuring mindfulness, the need for training business educators as mindfulness facilitators, and the contextualisation of mindfulness in contemporary business topics such as wellbeing, sustainability, diversity, and artificial intelligence. Part Three: How provides case studies and scripted resources for immediate use and implementation in extra-curricular or co-curricular activities to design mindfulness-based modules and courses, to introduce mindfulness coaching as part of pastoral care and staff development, and to develop mindfulness-driven business education strategies.

This is an ideal book for those in business education looking to use mindfulness to develop future managers and leaders.

Christine Rivers is Professor of Mindfulness and Business Education at Surrey Business School, University of Surrey, UK.

NEW DIRECTIONS IN BUSINESS EDUCATION

Mindfulness and Business Education
Developing self-aware future leaders – A practical guide
Christine Rivers

MINDFULNESS AND BUSINESS EDUCATION

Developing self-aware future leaders – A practical guide

Christine Rivers

LONDON AND NEW YORK

Designed cover image: Getty Images

First published 2025
by Routledge
4 Park Square, Milton Park, Abingdon, Oxon OX14 4RN

and by Routledge
605 Third Avenue, New York, NY 10158

Routledge is an imprint of the Taylor & Francis Group, an informa business

© 2025 Christine Rivers

The right of Christine Rivers to be identified as author of this work has been asserted in accordance with sections 77 and 78 of the Copyright, Designs and Patents Act 1988.

All rights reserved. No part of this book may be reprinted or reproduced or utilised in any form or by any electronic, mechanical, or other means, now known or hereafter invented, including photocopying and recording, or in any information storage or retrieval system, without permission in writing from the publishers.

Trademark notice: Product or corporate names may be trademarks or registered trademarks, and are used only for identification and explanation without intent to infringe.

British Library Cataloguing-in-Publication Data
A catalogue record for this book is available from the British Library

ISBN: 978-1-032-63742-6 (hbk)
ISBN: 978-1-032-63748-8 (pbk)
ISBN: 978-1-032-63746-4 (ebk)

DOI: 10.4324/9781032637464

Typeset in Times New Roman
by Taylor & Francis Books

In the interest of protecting their anonymity, all students have been given a pseudonym.

CONTENTS

List of illustrations ... xii

An introduction to mindfulness and business education ... 1
Intention of the book ... 1
Three parts: Why, What, and How ... 1
Mindfulness is a choice ... 3

PART I
Why mindfulness and business education? ... 5

1 Mindfulness – Friend or enemy? ... 7
   1.1 How do you feel about mindfulness? ... 7
   1.2 The mindfulness relationship ... 11
   1.3 Foundations of mindfulness ... 14
   1.4 McMindfulness, thin, or thick mindfulness ... 20
   Chapter 1 in a nutshell… ... 22

2 The marriage of mindfulness and business education: Pinstripe suit and jogging bottoms? ... 24
   2.1 Mindfulness in, as, of education ... 26
   2.2 VUCA and mindfulness – toughen up or soften down ... 28
   2.3 Mindfulness and leadership in business education ... 30
   2.4 Contemplative and embodied leadership ... 33
   Chapter 2 in a nutshell… ... 36

PART II
What to consider in the marriage of mindfulness and business education — 39

3 Purpose, measuring, and pedagogy — 41
   3.1 Purpose of mindfulness and business education — *42*
   3.2 Measuring effectiveness of mindfulness in business school classroom — *46*
   3.3 Facilitation: Skills, knowledge, and ethics — *48*
   3.4 Educational concepts for mindfulness and business education — *52*
   Chapter 3 in a nutshell… — *54*

4 Contextualising mindfulness and contemporary business topics — 58
   4.1 Employee wellbeing and mindfulness — *58*
   4.2 Sustainability and mindfulness — *59*
   4.3 DEI and mindfulness — *61*
   4.4 Artificial intelligence and mindfulness — *62*
   Chapter 4 in a nutshell… — *65*

PART III
How to bring mindfulness and business education to life — 69

5 Mindfulness as extracurricular activity — 71
   5.1 Engagement and commitment challenge — *71*
   5.2 'Good Enough' – leading with compassion: Case study — *73*
   5.3 'Good Enough': Resources — *75*
   5.4 'Good Enough': Considerations — *81*
   Chapter 5 in a nutshell… — *82*

6 Embedding mindfulness at programme/course level — 84
   6.1 Personal and professional development streams — *84*
   6.2 'Enrich Your Study Life': Case study — *85*
   6.3 'Enrich Your Study Life': Resources — *86*
   6.4 Consideration for programme/course level integration — *99*
   Chapter 6 in a nutshell… — *100*

7 Embedding mindfulness at module level and for assessment 102

   7.1 Success and mindfulness for future leaders *103*
   7.2 Self-awareness and mindfulness for future leaders *106*
   7.3 Self-care and mindfulness for future leaders *108*
   7.4 Assessing students' mindfulness skills *110*
   Chapter 7 in a nutshell… *113*

8 Mindfulness coaching and business education 116

   8.1 Coaching in business education *117*
   8.2 Mindfulness coaching *118*
   8.3 Mindfulness coaching for business students *120*
   8.4 Mindfulness coaching for business educators *126*
   Chapter 8 in a nutshell… *129*

9 Mindfulness-driven business education strategy 131

   9.1 Strategy means choice *131*
   9.2 Developing a business education strategy with intention and discernment *132*
   9.3 Adopting mindfulness language *134*
   9.4 Foundations of mindfulness and business education strategy *135*
   Evaluating the lived experience – Mindfulness of Dharma *141*
   Chapter 9 in a nutshell… *142*

Index *146*

ILLUSTRATIONS

Figures

5.1	Tree pose (variations)	78
5.2	Warrior Three (variations)	79

Tables

1.1	Overview of fourth foundation of mindfulness based on Goldstein (2013)	20
2.1	The role of mindfulness in education (derived from Ergas and Hadar, 2019)	27
2.2	Comparison of VUCA frameworks	29
2.3	Leadership periods, eras, and school over time	31
3.1	Mindfulness environments and indexes adopted from Chiang and Sumell (2019)	46
5.1	Retreat structure 'Good Enough'	74
6.1	Sutra questions and statements	98

AN INTRODUCTION TO MINDFULNESS AND BUSINESS EDUCATION

Intention of the book

You will have had your reasons for picking up this book. You might even have asked why do we need a book about mindfulness and business education? Isn't it hard enough to engage students and ensure they learn all they can to leave university qualified? Shouldn't we try to get the core business right instead of introducing concepts such as mindfulness into our day-to-day work? These are all valid questions and perhaps after reading this book, you will have some answers to those questions.

Before I start, I would like to share my intention for the book: The intention for this book is to be a guide for those of us who are passionate about developing self-aware, responsible future leaders or who want to change the world through business education. Thus, this book is not about mindfulness theory or conceptual pedagogies that cannot be implemented in business school environments. This book is about sharing practice, experience, and evidence about how mindfulness and business education are intrinsically interwoven and how one cannot do without the other.

Author's note: Throughout the book I will use the term business educator as an umbrella term to refer to any educators or teaching-focused staff who teach or facilitate learning of business and management related subjects. Similarly, I use the term business students. Subjects include but are not limited to: management, finance, accounting, marketing, entrepreneurship, human resources, tourism, events, economics. Educators includes teaching-intensive faculty, professors in practice and associates. Academics combine all faculty.

Three parts: Why, What, and How

The book is divided into three parts: Why, What, and How. Each part has been driven by fundamental questions business educators have been asking

DOI: 10.4324/9781032637464-1

for a while, and so far, it is unclear why we haven't either found a solution to these questions or tried something different to address them.

Why questions include but are not limited to: Why are we struggling to engage students? Why are so many of our students experiencing mental health issues? Why is group work perceived as painful? Why are leaders burning out?

Chapters 1 and 2 are concerned with the exploration of *why*. Chapter 1 starts by identifying our own connection and relationship with mindfulness before diving into the philosophy and foundations of mindfulness and discussing the concepts of McMindfulness, thin, and thick mindfulness. Chapter 2 proposes the marriage of mindfulness and business education. It draws on the history of business school, discusses the preposition of mindfulness as *in, of, as,* and *and* alliance, before outlining the environment future leaders are going to operate in, which warrants the marriage and the need for contemplative and embodied leadership models.

As I establish why we need to bring mindfulness practices and knowledge into business education as an alliance, we look at what we know and need to strengthen this alliance and implement it. *What* questions include but are not limited to: What is the purpose of marrying mindfulness and business education? What teaching skills and pedagogies are needed to deliver such education adequately? And what can we learn from measuring students' mindfulness levels? Furthermore, what topics align with mindfulness that we are already concerned with in business education?

Chapters 3 and 4 aim to address *what* questions. Chapter 3 looks at purpose, measuring mindfulness in the business school classroom and facilitation skills and education concepts we can use to frame our approach. Chapter 4 contextualises mindfulness within business topics we are already discussing in the business school classroom such as wellbeing, sustainability, diversity, equality and inclusion, and artificial intelligence.

The first two parts *Why* and *What* provide foundational knowledge and hopefully clarity concerning the need for this alliance. The third part of the book is dedicated to *How* this can be achieved. Chapters 5 to 9 are practical and experiential guides. Every chapter draws on my own and others research and experience in the field. But most importantly each chapter provides concrete case studies and resources (verbatim scripts and coaching question sets) that one can adapt to suit students' needs.

How questions include but are not limited to: How shall we embed mindfulness in business schools, as extracurricular, at programme/course level, as part of modules or as stand-alone modules? How useful is mindfulness coaching for business education purposes? How can we develop a mindfulness-driven business education strategy?

Chapter 5 dives into mindfulness and extra-curricular activities in the business school context. It starts by discussing engagement and commitment as two integral components for success. A case study and resources are included to support business educators utilising the materials in their own business school environment and are suitable to be offered as an extra-curricular activity or workshop.

Chapter 6 explores embedding mindfulness at programme/course level, in particular the integration of mindfulness as part of personal and professional development streams. A concrete case study and resources are provided to support its integration.

Chapter 7 outlines how mindfulness can be part of a module and its assessment strategy without explicitly referring to mindfulness. Concepts of success, self-awareness and self-care engage students in a self-exploration journey that moves from education to evocation, from authority to autonomy.

Chapter 8 shares insights and experiences of mindfulness coaching as part of business education. The chapter briefly summarises the concept and nature of coaching and mindfulness coaching specifically before focusing on mindfulness coaching for students that is relevant to personal tutoring and student peer-to-peer coaching and, finally, discusses the value of mindfulness coaching for business educators.

Chapter 9 provides ideas and direction for devising a mindfulness-driven business education strategy. Strategy as choice, intention and discernment, mindfulness language, and the applicability of the four foundations of mindfulness – the business school as an eco-system body – are the core topics of this final chapter.

Mindfulness is a choice

For me mindfulness is a way of being that we consciously choose. Through practice we can cultivate becoming more mindful, becoming who we are and living with intention. Yoga, meditation, breathwork, qigong, journaling, motivational coaching are tools to honour our choice, to cultivate a way of being, and we can use these tools to share this choice with our students and support them on their journey towards becoming self-aware, responsible future leaders.

Mindfulness is not a cure and not a solution to any of the challenges we might face in business education and beyond. However, in the words of Jon Kabat-Zinn mindfulness might be our only choice to address the challenges future leaders will face.

The good news is that mindfulness is free and accessible to all of us. We just need to learn how to use this tool. I like to refer to mindfulness as awareness intelligence because it is an innate awareness, which we seem to have forgotten. We have lost touch with how to be mindful with ourselves and others. We are easily distracted, eager to please others, always on the hunt for the golden nugget – happiness. Although we all know the saying 'Happiness is not a destination; it is a journey and a state of mind,' we still believe that we can *get* happiness through external gratification. So, what if we, business educators can use mindfulness practices to support students' personal and professional learning journeys with the goal of developing self-aware future leaders? What if we can transform learning and teaching to become a space for exploration of and reflection on the Self in alignment with business subjects? How would business education and therefore *doing* business change? How would the world be like?

Maybe you think this is unrealistic and ambitious. Maybe you think, *But this is not the world we live in.* You are right it is ambitious, and the main goal of corporates is often not to be mindful but to make profit. Yet, it is our choice. We can put our heads in the sand and carry on with same old, same old, or we can embrace something new and start transforming business education right here, right now in our own business schools and in the classroom.

Choice is a superpower. We, as business educators, have the skills and knowledge to equip future leaders with the *right* knowledge, *right* skills, and *right* tools to make *right* decisions and *right* choices that benefit society. I believe this is our duty and responsibility as business schools and educators and why we need this marriage of mindfulness knowledge and practice with business education.

Namaste,
Christine Rivers, PhD
Professor of Mindfulness and Business Education

PART I
Why mindfulness and business education?

1
MINDFULNESS – FRIEND OR ENEMY?

1.1 How do you feel about mindfulness?

I don't like the word mindfulness. I don't have time for mindfulness stuff. – are common statements when I share my passion for teaching and researching mindfulness with the academic community or work with students. It might seem counterintuitive to start a book about mindfulness with two negative statements about mindfulness. Whatever your reason for picking up this book up, I am not withholding the fact that mindfulness and business schools are not a natural marriage. If you are serious about infusing mindfulness into the curriculum and business school culture, you are more likely to experience rejection, suspicion, and judgment than support. While I was fortunate to have supportive line managers and therefore experienced less of a struggle to bring mindfulness to business education, I am aware that others might not have the privilege of such a welcoming environment. However, that does not mean that I did not have debates about what mindfulness is, what it is not, and whether it benefits business school life. The answer to the latter question is yes, and while you might face barriers initially, I encourage you to keep going. There is a reason you feel that there is a need, and you are absolutely right. Mindfulness is not our enemy; mindfulness is our friend, and the more we can create an appetite for mindfulness to become part of what we do as educators, scholars, and colleagues, the more likely we will be able to make that change happen. It is ambitious and it will take time, but it will be worth it in the end. Whether you seek to introduce mindfulness gradually, use it as a coaching tool with students and academic colleagues in your business school, or you want to make mindfulness a strategic pillar in your business school education policy, I first invite you to explore your own relationship with mindfulness, your story, your belief, and your commitment.

It took me a while to identify my relationship with mindfulness and to understand what *mindfulness* is and what it is not, philosophically, conceptually, and practically – because mindfulness was not a concept that featured greatly in my early career life. It can also feel daunting to dive into an area or topic and bring it into an environment where there might be preconceptions. It takes courage. I can confidently say from my own experience that it is worthwhile to be the outsider, the nerd, the mindfulness person because the rewards are far greater. Courage distinguishes one educator from another, the courage to offer future leaders a different perspective to think, feel and do business.

Three points are important and fundamental as we start this journey. First, while it is believed that mindfulness is rooted in Buddhism, mindfulness is not a religion. If we take a look at religions and spiritual traditions, all demonstrate core principles of mindfulness. Terminology and context might differ but all religions, to various extents, showcase mindfulness living. However, mindfulness can be practised in a secular way too. In principle, there is no need to refer to religious texts, yet I believe it is helpful to acknowledge roots and share origins, while at the same time remaining inclusive.

The second point I would make is that mindfulness is not a cure for suffering. Both exist, and we can choose to either be and live mindfully or to suffer. All human life contains some degree of suffering, which can be experienced on physical, mental, emotional, and psychological levels. In general, an experience that provokes suffering is usually described on a scale that ranges from unpleasant all the way to unbearable. The purpose of mindfulness practice is to identify suffering and utilise insights in such a way as to reduce one's suffering but, even more so, to learn to live with suffering in the present moment and to learn to live in a mindful way to enrich one's life in the long term, which in turn eases suffering naturally. The practice of mindfulness is a process of continuous experiential learning and learning to make peace with suffering. The sooner students can learn tools to address their own suffering and tap into their awareness intelligence the more likely they are to choose a mindful path and create a more just reality for themselves and others. Robin Sharma wrote in *The Monk Who Sold His Ferrari: Everything Is Created Twice, First in the Mind and Then in Reality* (Sharma, 2003).

My third point refers to the debate about whether mindfulness is a state of mind or a personality trait. Langer (2017) proclaims that mindfulness is a cognitive task associated with creativity and does not require enhancement through meditation practices. Mindfulness is perceived as a stable trait, and therefore someone has open awareness or a lack of it. In contrast, Goodman et al. (2017) highlight that mindfulness can be cultivated and individuals have the capacity to develop such a state of mind through mindfulness practices such as meditation. I believe that all beings (humans and animals) have an innate awareness intelligence, which we refer to as mindfulness and which exists all the time like the sky is always blue above the clouds. At our core, our deepest desire is to be happy, content, and live in harmony at work and at home. Mindfulness is all around us, within us, and surrounds us. Goldstein (2013, p. xiii) relates that the founder of the Duke Integrative Medicine programme at Duke University, Jeffrey Brantley, MD, put it this way: 'Mindfulness is at the core of everything we do.' We all have the capacity to be mindful (Brown & Ryan, 2003). Some have learned to access and use this intelligence more than others while growing up. Therefore, mindfulness is a trait and a state of mind at the same time. For some it might be dormant until awakened (Marques, 2010). Understanding that enabled me to keep going and pushing for mindfulness to be integrated into business school life, to stand up for what I believe in even though it feels like rolling a stone up a hill at times. What makes it worth it is when, from time to time, others help to roll the stone with me and we can experience the journey together.

The good news is that, alongside suspicion and misunderstanding, there is also an openness and curiosity in embracing mindfulness in business education to support the development and growth of business school faculty and students. This openness and curiosity are driven by an increase in popular culture mindfulness books written by academics and practitioners alike who have experienced the benefits of incorporating mindfulness in organisations and the workplace and have interviewed C-Suite folk about their experience of using mindfulness to manage stress, burnout and increase performance. Books such as *Mindful Leadership* (Gonzalez, 2012), *Mindful Work* (Gelles, 2015), and *Steps towards A Mindful Organization* (Mielke, 2021) have positively influenced the rise and interest in the subject as part of learning and development programmes, leadership training, and executive coaching over the past decade. While there seems to be robust evidence from industry, business schools remain hesitant to embed mindfulness in the curriculum or school strategy even though scientific-based mindfulness research has shown the benefits of mindfulness in terms of improving performance (Gardner & Moore, 2007), well-being (Carruthers & Hood, 2011), and relationships at work (Reb & Atkins, 2015; Reina et al., 2023). I believe that the reason for a rather slow adoption of mindfulness in business education is the fact the first two statements I opened this chapter with are still firmly present and true, and they govern whether one rejects, accepts, or embraces mindfulness as a concept and practice.

Let's attend to the first statement *I don't like the word mindfulness*. At first glance it indicates a rejection, but it also raises a question: *What do you not like about the word mindfulness?* The statement refers to the word rather than the concept or idea of mindfulness itself. While one could just accept the statement as is, as a curious person I see an opportunity to dive deeper into the conversation about what the word mindfulness and also the concept of mindfulness means to the person expressing the dislike. In my work as personal tutor and executive coach, these conversations, more often than not, have led to deep explorations and curiosity about the theory and practice of mindfulness. I like to share the following example that is still fondly in my memory.

Most of the time when students come to see us, it is because they are experiencing a challenge of some kind, academic or personal. I was personal tutor to an undergraduate student, called Ollie. Ollie is English and had left home for the first time. It was the beginning of the academic year – a rainy day, cold and windy, proper English autumn weather. When Ollie arrived at my office, he was soaked through. He sat down on the chair, and I offered him a cup of tea. We just sat there for a moment until I asked him how he was doing. The answer was short and what I usually receive from my teenage son, a dry and quiet *Okay*. I shared with him what my role involves and asked if there was anything he would like to add. I could not shake the idea that there was something off. He just shook his head, and we entered a longer period of silence, until he asked if he could just sit there. I also replied *Okay*. After a while, he said that he felt lonely and homesick and that he went to the wellbeing centre to speak to someone, but he didn't feel that it worked for him. He got agitated and cross because supposedly they suggested he write down his thoughts and become mindful of how he feels, how he gets up in the morning and so on. He finished by saying that he hates mindfulness stuff. I took a deep breath and thought *Oh boy, you came to the right office*. I asked him what he hated so much about mindfulness. He could not explain it and diverted from my question. Ollie shared that the one thing he missed the most was his dog. His dog, Bear, had been his companion since he was a little boy; he spent every minute with him. Bear died the evening before, and Ollie felt like a part of him died too. He felt guilty for not being with his dog at that moment, Ollie felt like he owed him because Bear was always there for him unconditionally, and now he was not sure how to study and engage with his peers while feeling that way. We talked about guilt, forgiveness, and death and how these states affect our day-to-day. I drew on my mindfulness knowledge and invited him to join me for some breathwork and gently moved him into a short, guided meditation fully knowing what he said before. I centred it around the feeling of sadness (the second foundation of mindfulness), the impermanence of life and experience, and how to be with and then shift from unpleasant to pleasant feelings. In that moment Ollie gave himself permission to be vulnerable and I provided the space. In the end, we sat for a while in silence, and he said: 'Thank you. Maybe I don't hate mindfulness, maybe I just didn't know what it is and how it could help me.' We never spoke about the session; we let it go. A couple of years later I received a LinkedIn message that read:

> *Christine, I wanted to thank you for the session you did with me when I was studying at Surrey. I learned to forgive myself and to be kinder to myself. I guess more mindful ☺. It was so helpful throughout my studies and now that I am working with so many different people I share it too. Maybe you can come and give a talk about how to be more mindful?*

And so I did, and we have stayed in touch since.

Ollie's story has become one of my examples, I share with students who ask about the benefits of being mindful for their studies and working life. They are intrigued about how they might be more successful, better leaders and managers. Throughout these explorations it becomes apparent that mindfulness is perceived as an intangible and unmeasurable thing that requires knowledge and practice and perhaps even spiritual commitment. In these conversations I ask my students what their perception, understanding, and relationship with the subject of their study is now (e.g. business management, marketing, finance) and what it was before they started? This question helps them to understand that mindfulness is just like studying a specific subject. The more you engage in it the clearer, more useful, and more applicable it becomes. I share that mindfulness is accessible to all of us regardless of backgrounds, abilities, aptitude, or knowledge. The question I am asked in return is: Does this mean that we human beings are innately mindful and, if this is the case, why are we not mindful all the time? While answering this question in detail is beyond the scope of this book, I believe that we have the ability to be mindful (to act, feel, and think mindfully) with ourselves and others at all times, but it is hard to maintain that. We will return to this question when we have spent some time on what mindfulness means.

To emphasise the importance of first exploring our own relationship with mindfulness before conceptually defining it, I would like to share my own story about my relationship with mindfulness, which for a long time was framed by the two statements that open this chapter.

1.2 The mindfulness relationship

I grew up in Austria, in a Catholic family. My parents both enjoyed going to church and sharing their morals and values. We had many conversations about what is right and wrong, what constitutes a good citizen, and what society expects. It is fair to say that I was not an easy child. I was boisterous, challenging and extremely curious, a little rebel most of the time. It is no surprise that a sentence I would often hear, was: *You need to be more mindful. Du must ein bisschen achtsamer sein.* The German word for mindfulness is *Achtsamkeit*, which basically means to pay more attention to actions and words in relation to others and less to oneself. A word closely related to *Achtsamkeit* is *Achtung*, which one would shout in case of emergency to get someone's attention.

My association with mindfulness was therefore mostly related to situations where I was not acting mindfully towards others. I needed to be reminded a lot. Mostly about the fact that I was acting wrongly or not in line with societal expectations, morals, and norms. After a while, I did not hear the sentence – it became noise; at best I would roll my eyes in an attempt at acknowledging it (again not very mindful). Therefore, my connotation of mindfulness was rooted in an experience that would naturally reject anything related to it because it triggered a feeling and thoughts of not being good enough, not doing it right, and alienating people around me. There was little understanding at the time of how such behaviour might be a reflection of my own relationship with myself. Of course, this was not the intention of my parents. They tried their best to bring up a good citizen, who was mindful of others.

At the time, I was not aware that my belief of what mindfulness means and is would determine every step I took, every decision I made. I was unaware of the fact that my own connotations of mindfulness shaped my rejection of and aversion to yoga, meditation, or anything related to finding stillness and silence, being present, and just being. In fact, my relationship to self was distorted. Body and mind were separated, which led to eating disorders and substance use. However, over the years there were attempts to rekindle that relationship. I studied communications and anthropology and became interested in indigenous wisdom and knowledge systems. I started reading about Buddhism and went to the occasional yoga class and the meditation temple. But I was too scared to face myself and quickly gave up. Interestingly, my deepest desire was to be a mindful person and to love who I am. That insight only came to me when I hit rock bottom, when I had nothing left, when I felt depressed and lonely despite being successful and surrounded by loving family and friends. My suffering, which I denied for so long, became so strong that the only way to get out of it was to go inwards. I felt a strong need to quiet my mind. At the start of the pandemic, a friend recommended yoga. My first reaction was rejection, and I even rolled my eyes probably. But there was a voice inside me that pushed and asked: What is the worst that can happen? I committed to a 30-day online programme. In the beginning, my body and mind were fighting, and over time, they found peace. Yoga and meditation were some of the tools I used to become mindful with myself. On this journey, I was able to drop my old beliefs about mindfulness and rekindle my relationship. The benefits I experienced were profound. I made an effort to be present with people and focus my attention on the tasks I was doing instead of trying to juggle three things at once. As a result, I felt less stressed, my mind calmed down, and I developed a deep curiosity for engaging in tasks and observing my body and mind being part of it. Life itself became joyful. I started to engage with like-minded people and found that I was not the only one seeking inner peace and mindful living, particularly at work. Both, students and staff approached me to talk about how to be more mindful, self-caring, and self-loving. The pandemic changed us of course but it kick-started a new journey. Despite my senior leadership roles in the business school, I started to offer mindfulness workshops focused on specific topics (e.g. leadership, assessment stress, study focus) and facilitated free weekly yoga and meditation sessions. My passion for sharing these tools and supporting young minds and colleagues grew, particularly as people participating in these sessions shared the positive impact of these interventions.

Thus, the first step towards bringing mindfulness into your learning and teaching is to ask: *What is my relationship with mindfulness?* I invite you to write down whatever comes up. You might find that your thoughts are judgmental and all over the place. You might find that an inner dialogue occurs about what mindfulness is or not. In fact, mindfulness is often referred to as a fuzzy subject. Let it be, and sit with it for a moment. This is part of the journey; it is essential and necessary to allow the mind to go wild, ask questions, become curious. Idowu Koyenikan (2016) in his book *Wealth for All*, said: 'The mind is just like a muscle – the more you exercise it, the stronger it gets and the more it can expand.' Now that you have written down your interpretation of mindfulness and your relationship with it, let us explore the background of mindfulness a little more.

There are many definitions for mindfulness, which emphasises the fuzziness of the term and also the dissension among scholars. I can see relevance in multiple definitions but the one that I prefer to use when I introduce mindfulness is derived from the Pali word *Sati*. In Buddhist tradition *Sati* has many meanings and functions, and all have the purpose of improving one's life, seeing clearly, growing wisdom. Directly translated, *Sati* means to *remember*. Joseph Goldstein (2013, p. 231, one of the influential figures who brought mindfulness to the west, shared this: 'It's not hard to be mindful. It just takes training to remember to be mindful.' This phrase hits the nail on the head and answers the question raised by the above: Why do we struggle to be mindful all the time? Goldstein's statement implies two important aspects. In order to remember something, we need to be able to access what it is we want to remember. This requires knowledge about the process of remembering itself, which we rarely question because as soon as we set our attention on something we can initiate the process of remembering. Second, preceding the need to remember and putting our attention to something is an intention. There will be a reason why we focus our attention on a specific aspect. Maybe we just need to recall information, or we need to apply knowledge in different contexts or to satisfy needs. Attention and intention play crucial roles in the process of becoming more mindful. In my experience of working with undergraduate and postgraduate students in business school contexts, the process of remembering through paying attention to the connection and communication between their body and mind in the pursuit of understanding themselves better and feeling happier is like a Eureka moment, and it is all that is required to plant the seed.

Interestingly, to remember is also the first cognitive domain of Bloom's revised taxonomy (Krathwohl, 2002), which we frequently use in higher education to design learning, teaching, and assessment units. The original taxonomy of educational objectives referred to this first domain as *Knowledge* and Bloom (1956) described it as the cognitive process that involves recalling of different types of something (e.g. information, patterns, structures, or specifics). This cognitive process is performed by the mind. Mindfulness of the mind is referred to as the third foundation of mindfulness in Buddhist tradition and psychology (Feldman and Kuyken, 2019).

1.3 Foundations of mindfulness

There are four foundations of mindfulness also known as the *satipatthana*: (1) mindfulness of the body, (2) mindfulness of feeling tone, (3) mindfulness of mental states, and (4) mindfulness of our experience of the world. Thus, mindfulness is not just a cognitive process, it is a whole-body experience, and what we learn to remember when we practice mindfulness is to experience the here and now. This experience is being aware of what is happening in the body, the mind, and around us in the present moment.

This section aims to give a basic understanding of Joseph Goldstein's detailed descriptions of the foundations of mindfulness rather than provide a deep dive. For further reading Joseph Goldstein's (2013) book *Mindfulness – A Practical Guide to Awakening*, is a great resource to explore each foundation in great length and depth. This section gives an overview of the four foundations of mindfulness. However further reading is advised to dive deeper into each of them. The four foundations of mindfulness are rooted in Buddhist psychology and are understood as the route map from suffering to flourishing (Feldman and Kuyken, 2019). The purpose of the foundations is to identify any kind and intensity of physical, mental, or emotional suffering and reduce it through mindfulness practice. Our senses enable us to experience the body, the mind, and the world around us.

First foundation of mindfulness – Mindfulness of the body

The body is a vessel, and we can experience and learn to know the body as the body in stillness or movement – lying, standing, sitting, or walking. The point is to bring awareness to the body without judgment. That is the difference between mindfully engaging with the body or not. For instance, you might stand in front of the mirror criticising the body, which increases your suffering through judgment. Or you can stand in front of the mirror and look at the body without judgment – as it is. Noticing the shape, the skin tone, the temperature of the body by touching it. While thoughts might arise, you have the option not to follow the thoughts. You have the choice to let them float by. This approach of observing the body non-judgmentally, as it is there and then, takes time and practice, as our relationship with the body is complex and paradoxical. In Western society, we have learned to foster an over-identification with the physical body and its appearance, while at the same time we are disconnected from the body too. We have forgotten how to experience the body as it is in the present moment. Mindfulness of the body is about cultivating that present moment experience. We only seem to pay attention and be present with the body if something hurts or is unpleasant – when we suffer. Therefore, our relationship with our body predominantly exists in a negative state of being supported by similar judging thoughts. This relationship is also reinforced through daily and regular media consumption feeding our suffering. Breaking out of this cycle is challenging, and this is where mindfulness practice has its place in paying attention to different parts of the body at one time so we can reframe our relationship with the body, become aware of it as it is. Cultivating such awareness allows us to connect with self as we learn to listen to the body and appreciate the body without fear, aversion, or expectation. The body is full of wisdom and information. Yoga and meditation are great tools to start to deepen our relationship with the body mindfully. There are three meditation techniques I regularly use with students, which are particularly helpful in cultivating mindfulness of the body and accessing that wisdom: body scan, body part contemplation, and breath work. Below is a short description of each and what insights we can gain by utilising these techniques. A scripted version of how to integrate these techniques can be found in the third part of this book, *How*.

Body scan

Body scans can be experienced lying, standing, or sitting down. There are many variations of body scans available to practise. It is a form of guided meditation where the teacher, after settling the participants into the space, directs attention towards a particular body part, usually the toes or the crown of the head. Attention is given to the sensation. A teacher might also use a visualisation technique, such as golden light that travels through the body parts. The experience can be relaxing and soothing for the body and mind. Body scans are usually performed with eyes closed.

Insights from a body scan are wide reaching and differ from person to person depending on the relationship one has with one's body. However, most people learn that the body is not a fixed vessel, but a place where processes occur, experiences come and go, and change happens. It is a great way and representation for life and the impermanence of everything in life.

Body part contemplation

An alternative to the body scan is to focus on one particular body part, such as hands, feet, or face. In this scenario, the person contemplating has their eyes open and stares at the particular body part while being guided by the teacher to access and sharpen awareness. During contemplation, the person can create a deep connection to the body part, which in turn can change their perception of it.

Appreciation and gratitude are two of the main insights reported. For instance, as we are using our hands to type emails or write reports and essays, we are unaware of the tasks our hands perform, how they are in constant motion. Only when we experience pain or unusual sensations do we pay attention. Equally each finger has a role to play, and only if we were to lose one, would we notice its importance.

Breathing and qualities of the breath

We often think that breathing only takes place in the upper part of the body but if we pay close attention, we can notice the whole body breathing. Breathing is an anchor and often the first point of contact one has with practising mindfulness of the body. There are many breathing techniques which are commonly referred to as breath work. The simplest is to direct one's attention to the qualities of the breath while sitting or lying down. I like to guide my students through five qualities of breathing before diving into counting breath exercises. The first quality is to notice the temperature of the air coming in through the nose as we breathe in and the temperature of the air as we breathe out. The second quality is to observe where the body breathes, into the chest or into the belly, whether the action of breathing can be felt in the back or only in the front. The third quality refers to the sound of the breath. For some the sound of the inhale and exhale might be familiar; for others, hearing the sound of one's own breath is new and strange. The fourth quality refers to observing the rhythm of the breath. This includes noticing the length of the inhale, the little pause, and the length of the exhale, followed by a little pause. The fifth quality of the breath focuses on the sensations experienced in the moment of breathing, which often leads to entering the second foundation of mindfulness: mindfulness of feeling tone.

Breath exercises can help one to see the connection between body and mind clearly, and they again emphasise the fact that nothing is permanent, but rather it is in constant motion. On the other hand, after breath work one can experience stillness and silence settling in for a while, which is one of the experiences most students and people at work long for, and it can lead to sustained awareness. Breath exercises are a good starting point to support students during assessment periods and to learn to calm body and mind by focusing on the breath.

Second foundation of mindfulness – Mindfulness of feeling tone

Any sensations we experience can be categorised as pleasant, unpleasant, or neutral. These are the three feelings tones mindfulness works with as a starting point to identify what is going on. Feeling tone is highly subjective and depends on an individual's past experience and learning. For instance, if my experience with spiders is negative and I learned to kill spiders when I see them in the house, then the feeling tone is unpleasant. If I learned to appreciate spiders and put them back outside, then my feeling tone might be neutral or pleasant when I see one in my bedroom. Most of the time, we do not assess our feeling tone; we just react, and it is that reactivity that can hold us back from being curious, open-minded, and mindful towards ourselves. Becoming aware of the feeling tone through meditation is helpful to fine-tune our actions, words, and thoughts, and it enables us to change behaviours and attitudes towards experiences and events in the future.

In the world of work, it is paramount to be able to be comfortable with unpleasant experiences so that we can react more mindfully towards ourselves and others. Blame and aversion are often experienced by students, particularly in group work settings. If something did not go to plan, students can be quick to blame others or external circumstances, which is a coping mechanism to direct the unpleasant feeling elsewhere. Similarly, a lot of students avoid group work assessment so not to be exposed to the potential unpleasant event. It is often described as 'group work is painful.' Thus, mindfulness workshops that focus on feeling tone exploration can prepare students for group work scenarios and support them throughout team-based projects.

Third foundation of mindfulness – Mindfulness of the mind

The third foundation of mindfulness refers to mental and emotional states. It takes the second foundation of mindfulness, feeling tone, further. I would even say that the third foundation dissects feeling tone. For instance, we might experience an unpleasant feeling, which we can identify as unpleasant, but in order to work with it, we need to label it so that we can make sense of it. It is common for graduates to experience anxiety before a job interview, which is a complex emotional state (Feldman & Kuyken, 2019).

Our mental and emotional states have a profound impact on our mind. We experience reality through mental and emotional states, and we interpret, make sense, and respond based on those states. Therefore, the more aware we become of current mental and emotional states, the better we can manage challenges at work and at home. We can make informed decisions with clarity and intention. For instance, experiencing anxiety before a job interview can further be broken down into the thoughts and emotions that arise. Alongside feeling anxious, the thoughts might be judging and belittling resulting in the body experiencing stress and an elevated heart rate. In that moment, we are unable to see clearly and act in a way that is authentic.

However not all our mental and emotional states are always that obvious, and sometimes these states can also be conflicting, which results in rumination and long internal dialogues. Learning to bring awareness to mental and emotional states can help us to understand the impermanence of those states, gradually disempower them, and learn to be with such states without being all consumed. The mind is malleable, and mindfulness practice focused on mental and emotional state identification trains the mind to know which thoughts and emotions lead to a specific outcome. In 2022, I led mindfulness workshops for teenagers who were 14 years old in a UK community college to address their anxiety and stress around upcoming assessments. After the five-week programme, I asked the pupils if anything had changed or what was different now. One of the participants, Lucy said: '*I now know I do not have to be anxious all the time. I now know that it passes. I feel more in control of my thoughts.*' Lucy learned that her anxiety triggered negative thoughts and prevented her from sitting exams at times. Therefore, she felt that school was not for her because she felt controlled by her anxiety. Mindfulness practice gave her a toolbox to know herself better.

Fourth foundation of mindfulness – Mindfulness *of* Dharma

Joseph Goldstein (2013) refers to this fourth foundation as mindfulness of *Dhammas*. It is probably the most complex foundation of mindfulness, yet it is the one that most students find the most fascinating. Some refer to this fourth foundation as mindfulness of *Dhamma* (Pali) or mindfulness of *Dharma* (Sanskrit). I prefer to work with the latter, *Dharma*. Lowitz and Datta (2009) describe *Dharma* as the *underlying moral structure of the universe, the fundamental law of our nature* which each human carries within and which determines the path, everyday actions, thoughts, and words spoken. Sometimes *Dharma* is also translated as truth, duty, righteousness, or that which holds together. The Buddha, in his teachings, identified ways of living a truthful life (*Dharma*) by examining our suffering (*Dukkha*). Through examination, introspection, and interrogation, the concept of self can change. Examination leads to a person's truthful path. On this journey of our truthful path, we are confronted with obstacles, which can be referred to as hindrances and aggregates of clinging, which are part of the experience of suffering.

The Buddha shared five hindrances: desire, aversion, sloth and torpor, restlessness and worry, and doubt. It is natural to have desires, some are driven by our ego and others by our heart. Ego desires are mostly linked to material desires such a wanting a new car or a bigger house. Even if we fulfil these desires, suffering will continue, as it is never enough. Desires of the heart cannot be bought and cannot be fulfilled to such an extent that we get bored of them because they are seldom materialistic. What the heart desires leads to transformation from within, and the path becomes enjoyable because of it. Heart desires serve the greater good, the community, the people around us as much as they serve us. These desires are not end goals or things to possess, rather they are states of being we long for so we can release suffering. They are personal and yet universal, from learning to be patient, non-judgmental, joyful, accepting to feeling content. Through investigation the heart's desires will become clearer, and, on the journey, more hindrances might affect its seamless growth. We might experience aversion to people or situations that challenge us to stay true to ourselves, which in turn leads us to more suffering. Sloth and torpor, which refers to physical and mental lack of energy might also hold us back from practising being patient, content, or loving.

Restlessness and worry creep in and grab hold of our thoughts leading to doubt and negative emotions towards ourselves. Suffering is endless, and it might feel like a constant inner battle against those hindrances. However, through introspection and investigation, whether through meditation or yoga, for instance, we can learn to understand what is holding us back and we can identify what we are clinging on to that enables those hurdles to appear again and again.

The five aggregates of clinging – *khandhas* in Pali – affect our journey to the truth. Clinging means not wanting to let go or struggling to let go; some might even experience it as an inability to let go of what feels 'safe,' what we 'know' and are used to. We cling because we are scared of the unknown, yet 'people grow the most when they enter the zone of the unknown' (Sharma, 2003, p.117). In the West, we have certain ideals of how a female or male body is aesthetically pleasing and should therefore look. Advertising and media in general feed this ideal and condition our mind, appeal to our ego. We start to cling on the experience of material form; we imagine what it would feel like. We even believe that by wearing certain clothes, working in a certain firm we will get closer to that ideal. We cling on to feelings and perceptions of objects and places. In the end, we have created an illusion around us that is built on a desire fuelled by what we believe will end our suffering, and it might feel good for a while, and so we cling on to that experience. Some refer to the good old days. The more we cling the more suffering we experience.

This experience is only possible through our senses. Six internal (eye, ear, nose, tongue, body, mind) and six external sense spheres (odours, sounds, tastes, touch, mind objects) determine our day-to-day perception of life. The senses can cloud our judgment and infiltrate our perception, altering our reality. They can make us believe what is unattractive to be attractive, what is unsatisfactory to be satisfactory, what is unreal to be real, and what is not the self to be the self. It is also referred to as the wheel of conditioned existence (Wheel of Samsāra). In meditation, we attempt to remove this layer of illusion and connect to our awareness within us; that is our truthful path. In this moment of stillness and silence, we have the ability to clearly *see*, but it takes time and practice.

On this path of self-exploration and inner work, the Buddha shared four noble truths about suffering itself. the first noble truth is of suffering (*Dukkha*) itself. I would refer to it as the noticing and becoming aware of suffering taking place – acknowledging that suffering is part of life and experienced by all beings in one form or another, to lesser or greater degree. The second noble truth is to identify what the cause of one's suffering is. Perhaps it is the constant desire to become more, have more or the constant worry and doubt about not being good enough and meeting societal expectations. While there might be a list of causes, focusing on one at a time is recommended. The third noble truth is the acknowledgement of and commitment to cessation of suffering or the end to craving, desire, worry, and so on. The fourth noble truth is about the way we can take to stop our suffering, which refers to the eightfold path. Three factors mark the eightfold path: wisdom, morality, and concentration. On this journey, we learn to use our inner wisdom by identifying right view and right thought. This is supported by right speech, right action, and right livelihood, which are understood as morality factors. Finally, the right effort, right mindfulness, and right concentration are needed, too, on our way to the truth. Table 1.1 summarises the elements of mindfulness of *Dharma*.

1.4 McMindfulness, thin, or thick mindfulness

Ronald Purser is probably the best-known author and spokesperson to take a critical stance towards the celebrated mindfulness movement in the West, referring to mindfulness as a lubricant for capitalism and complicit with neo-liberalism (Purser, 2019). In his book *McMindfulness: How Mindfulness Became the New Capitalist Spirituality*, Purser is particularly critical about the way mindfulness is commercially exploited, without ethical or moral standards

TABLE 1.1 Overview of fourth foundation of mindfulness based on Goldstein (2013)

Five hindrances	*Desire, aversion, sloth and torpor, restlessness and worry, doubt*
Five aggregates of clinging (*khandhas* in Pali)	Clinging on to experience of material form (feet, belly, arms, head)
	Clinging on to feelings and perception of objects, self, places, time
	Clinging on to mental concepts
	Clinging on to experience itself
Six internal and external sense spheres	Internal senses – eye, ear, nose, tongue, body, mind
	External sense sphere – odours, sounds, tastes, touch, mind objects
	Wheel of conditioned existence (Wheel of Samsāra) hallucinations of perceptions refer to beliefs such as believing what is unattractive to be attractive, what is unsatisfactory to be happiness, what is impermanent to be permanent and what is not the self to be the self.
Seven factors for awakening	Mindfulness, investigation of *Dharmas*, energy, rupture, calm, concentration, equanimity
The four noble truths	First noble truth – Suffering (*Dukkha*)
	Second noble truth – The cause of suffering
	Third noble truth – Cessation of suffering
	Fourth noble truth – The way to cessation of suffering / the eightfold path
The eightfold path (three factors)	Wisdom factors – Right view, right thought
	Morality factors – Right speech, right action, right livelihood
	Concentration factors – Right effort, right mindfulness, right concentration

underpinning its adoption, with the sole purpose of profit making. Thus, his critique is much more about the lack of social and political aspects to how mindfulness is deployed within a capitalist world. One can understand that this approach sits in stark contrast with the Buddhist roots of mindfulness, where teachers give their time freely and offer mindfulness services for the greater good. Thus, the term *McMindfulness*, first introduced by Miles Neale, refers to mindfulness becoming a commodity, produced at scale for mass consumption, similar to McDonalds, which established a new industry worth billions. It may sound ironic, but a capitalist perspective is the approach most students are still taught in business schools today (Moratis & Melissen, 2022). We could argue that John Elkington's term 'triple bottom line' (Elkington, 2018), introduced nearly three decades ago, should have brought much needed change, away from a single bottom line, solely profit-driven business model to one that balances profit, people, and planetary needs. Yet the framework remained mostly conceptual with minor exceptions – businesses that embraced the idea of measuring the economic, social, and environmental value added from doing business. Most businesses continued to pursue the capitalist route with a strong focus on profit.

Another distinction of how mindfulness is utilised predominantly in educational settings has been offered by McCaw (2020): thin versus thick mindfulness. Thin mindfulness approaches are described as a tool for individual self-improvement, ethically neutral without social-critical framing and disconnected from its roots in Buddhism. Mindfulness packages are offered as a personal or professional development tool which is taught and practiced in secular way. This perspective is similar to Neale's and Purser's McMindfulness definition. In contrast, thick mindfulness approaches utilise and are embedded in Buddhist teachings to some extent. Facilitators recognise and acknowledge the heritage. Workshops are designed around the Buddha's teachings, with the purpose of improving individual wellbeing and health rather than focusing on increasing productivity to meet profit targets and putting responsibility for wellbeing solely onto individuals.

We could ask the question: How would the mindfulness industry have grown differently if business schools and organisations had abandoned the capitalist business model approach and pushed the triple bottom line to be the new normal? Perhaps mindfulness trainers would not charge thousands of pounds/dollars for one-day workshops. Perhaps mindfulness training in organisations would move away from solely blaming individuals for problems and instead utilise mindfulness to address systemic issues, because not all problems are down to an individual (e.g. stress and burn out can be personal but also a question of workload, expectations, and leadership). It is not too late to make a change. Mindfulness has the potential to have a long-term positive impact, not just on individuals, but also in bringing about profound social change (Purser, 2019). As business schools, major providers of business education and developers of future leaders, we are best placed to bring this change about. We have a responsibility to drive system change and to contribute to the creation of a healthier, more ethical, and more socially critical society.

Chapter 1 in a nutshell...

The word mindfulness usually sparks one of two reactions – aversion or invitation. Either reaction is usually informed by how we learned about mindfulness in the first place, in what context one was introduced to mindfulness or not. Understanding one's relationship with mindfulness is fundamental to developing leadership qualities. It is no longer a question of toughening up or softening our teaching to enable that. It is a question of how we as business educators can guide a new generation of leaders to acquire a new perspective towards leadership that is grounded in mindfulness; a perspective that incorporates the virtues of integrity, kindness, humility, responsibility, and respect towards oneself and others in the pursuit of creating a better, more just society and world. The question should rather be: Do we, as business educators, want to change the world? If so, and I would hope it is simply a unanimous yes, we need to start changing our own perspective and infuse mindfulness into learning and teaching.

Regardless of what we think individually, as business schools, we have a responsibility to equip future leaders with the knowledge, skills, and awareness to make decisions that have a long-term positive impact on people and our planet. We need to shift our focus. We need to let go of the *same old, same old* paradigm – successful leaders are data-driven, profit-oriented, and confident. Instead, we need to embrace developing future leaders who are skilled in balancing internal and external self-awareness, who act with integrity and humility, who respond with intention, and who can access their innate awareness in a way that benefits themselves and others equally. The goal is not necessarily to be mindful all the time, because there is a time to be present and a time to connect with the past and future. However, we need to enable future leaders to access their awareness intelligence so they can return to the present moment to make decisions that benefit businesses and society.

References

Bloom, B. S. (1956). *Taxonomy of educational objectives: The classification of educational goals: Handbook I, cognitive domain*. Longmans.

Brown, K. W., & Ryan, R. M. (2003). The benefits of being present: mindfulness and its role in psychological well-being. *Journal of Personality and Social Psychology*, 84(4), 822–848.

Carruthers, C., & Hood, C. D. (2011). Mindfulness and wellbeing. *Therapeutic Recreation Journal*, 3, 171–189.

Elkington, J. (2018). 25 years ago I coined the phrase "triple bottom line." Here's why it's time to rethink it. *Harvard Business Review*. https://hbr.org/2018/06/25-years-ago-i-coined-the-phrase-triple-bottom-line-heres-why-im-giving-up-on-it.

Feldman, C., & Kuyken, W. (2019). *Mindfulness: Ancient wisdom meets modern psychology*. Guilford Publications.
Gardner, F. L., & Moore, Z. E. (2007). *The psychology of enhancing human performance: The mindfulness-acceptance-commitment (MAC) approach*. Springer Publishing Company.
Gelles, D. (2015). *Mindful work: How meditation is changing business from the inside out*. Houghton Mifflin Harcourt.
Goldstein, J. (2013). *Mindfulness: A practical guide to awakening*. Sounds True.
Gonzalez, M. (2012). *Mindful leadership: The 9 ways to self-awareness, transforming yourself, and inspiring others*. John Wiley & Sons.
Goodman, M. S., Madni, L. A., & Semple, R. J. (2017). Measuring mindfulness in youth: Review of current assessments, challenges, and future directions. *Mindfulness*, 8, 1409–1420.
Koyenikan, I. (2016). *Wealth for all: Living a life of success at the edge of your ability*. Grandeur Touch.
Krathwohl, D. R. (2002). A revision of Bloom's taxonomy: An overview. *Theory into practice*, 41(4), 212–218.
Langer, E. J. (2017). Mindfulness and mindlessness. In J. O'Brien (Ed.), *The production of reality: Essays and readings on social interaction* (6th ed., pp. 110–115). Sage.
Lowitz, L., & Datta, R. (2009). *Sacred Sanskrit words: For yoga, chant, and meditation*. Stone Bridge Press.
Marques, J. F. (2010). Awakened leaders: Born or made? *Leadership & Organization Development Journal*, 31(4), 307–323.
McCaw, C. T. (2020). Mindfulness 'thick' and 'thin'—A critical review of the uses of mindfulness in education. *Oxford Review of Education*, 46(2), 257–278.
Mielke, F. (2021). *Steps towards a Mindful Organisation: Developing Mindfulness to Manage Unexpected Events*. Springer Gabler.
Moratis, L., & Melissen, F. (2022). Bolstering responsible management education through the sustainable development goals: Three perspectives. *Management Learning*, 53(2), 212–222.
Purser, R. (2019). *McMindfulness: How mindfulness became the new capitalist spirituality*. Repeater.
Reb, J., & Atkins, P. W. (2015). *Mindfulness in organizations: Foundations, research, and applications*. Cambridge University Press.
Reina, C. S., Kreiner, G. E., Rheinhardt, A., & Mihelcic, C. A. (2023). Your presence is requested: Mindfulness infusion in workplace interactions and relationships. *Organization Science*, 34(2), 722–753.
Sharma, R. (2003). *The monk who sold his Ferrari: A fable about fulfilling your dreams & reaching your destiny*. Jaico Publishing House.

2

THE MARRIAGE OF MINDFULNESS AND BUSINESS EDUCATION

Pinstripe suit and jogging bottoms?

Business education like mindfulness has the been subject of debate among scholars for over 100 years, particularly around what is taught and how business education should be taught. Business schools emerged out of arts and social sciences and, in particular, economics departments. The first successful business school (Wharton's School of Finance and Economy, 1881) focused on teaching economic history and taught students the needs of business. Wharton's received criticism about the lack of classical academic education and had to defend its position (Wren & Van Fleet, 1983) for years before flourishing. Wharton's recruited its first *business educators* from liberal arts departments at the University of Pennsylvania, who found it challenging to teach in the practical-oriented Wharton spirit. Two years later, in 1883, the University leadership hired educators who were more in tune with business subjects and the applied way of teaching these. However, the struggle continued for a while, with little funding and concerns of quality of scholarship being jeopardised in the University by Wharton's. Seven years later, the University of Chicago and University of California (Berkeley) followed suit. Slowly more business schools developed, and economic history was recognised as a subject discipline around 1925. Edwin F. Gay was an influential figure in this process. Gay was Professor and later Dean of Graduate School of Business Administration at Harvard University. Gay's teaching and research focused on real-world problem solving rather than academic theorising. Gay carried out a study with 38 members of AACSB (American Association of Collegiate Schools of Business) to determine how economic history was taught and integrated into the curriculum.

AACSB was founded in 1916 and was led by Gay and two other business school deans. A further fourteen schools were invited to join the group and first accreditations took place in 1919. From the beginning the group set standards to ensure excellence in business education was met and maintained. AACSB's intention was to help its members to share curriculum, faculty training, and reputational protection. The AACSB standards have since been revised several times to reflect the ongoing changes in the business education landscape. Geopolitical events (World Wars I and II) that took place in the early 20th century led to new subjects being taught in business schools, such as labour relations (Locke, 1982) and human behaviour in the workplace (Acton, 2023; Bruce & Nyland, 2011). Human relations and organisational behaviour were solidly integrated into business schools' curriculums. Donham, Dean of Harvard Business School (1919–1942), played a particular role in bring to the fore the need for businesses to act in a more socially responsible way, which was taught as part of organisational behaviour at the time. However, over the years, the focus at Harvard Business School shifted to finding solutions to management problems through quantitative measures, and many other business schools adopted similar research interests and incorporated those into courses. Since then, management as science has dominated what is taught and how teaching and learning takes place in most business schools. Science-based management transformed business education (Zeff, 2008).

The rise of business schools in America was not unnoticed by the rest of the world, and more business schools emerged in the early 20th century, which copied the American business school model and adopted learning materials from accredited top-tier business schools. The understanding was that business is business regardless of location, culture, or language. Accredited business schools became a symbol of producing outstanding graduates who were highly valued by industry. Accreditation functioned as a differentiator between top-tier and lower-tier schools and graduates. Accredited business schools enrolled students only on merit, and they were sought after by profitable companies. It became a competitive elite process. Those who graduated from the prestigious accredited schools took on well-paid managerial jobs. When the time came for them to hire new staff, they turned to graduates from the same business schools they went to. Students also chose business schools based on their reputation and the opportunities they offered after study rather than course offerings, content, or teaching provision (Acton, 2023; Spender, 2017). The first business school rankings introduced in 1987 heightened competition even more. In addition, reports published by the Ford and Carnegie Foundation, who worked with AACSB and informed the revision of standards, called for an increase in intellectual contribution by raising the quantity of outputs and quality of faculty. These reports led to business schools hiring academics based on research outputs rather than teaching skills. From there on quantifiable, measurable, and therefore teachable hard science replaced business history and philosophy in the curriculum and in research even though the outcomes of most studies were less relevant to real-world problem solving and therefore managerial or business practice (Spender, 2017; Bryant et al, 2022).

However, towards the end of the 20th century, influenced by geopolitical events once more, management education changed. To counter the rising neo-liberalist economy, entrepreneurship and leadership topics (King et al., 1990) found their way into the business school curriculum. Students welcomed the change of direction, and it led to an influx of applications for courses featuring or focusing on leadership, human resources, and entrepreneurship. The emergence of the more practice-oriented, real-world, less theory-based subjects stood in juxtaposition to economic theorising based on mathematical models, which still dominated. This dichotomy created tension and reignited the debate around the value of business school programmes, the value and relevance of business schools to society, and what business schools should and should not teach (Bennis and O'Toole, 2005). One point is certain, business schools as education providers have a responsibility to positively impact society, and business education has great potential to develop future leaders who have the ability to apply theory to practice and utilise data to inform decisions while leading with integrity and kindness. It is no longer a debate of pinstripe suits or jogging bottoms but of who can lead skilfully and mindfully.

Before diving deeper into what we should teach, I would like to establish the preposition of how mindfulness connects with education and business education in particular. Understanding its position within the context of business education either as an equal partner or muse changes the way we integrate it but also how we perceive its value and contribution.

2.1 Mindfulness in, as, of education

Ergas & Hadar (2019) published a systematic literature review in *Review of Education* that captured mindfulness research conducted in primary, secondary, and post-secondary education between 2002 and 2017. Their study revealed two interesting insights that seem to be helpful in understanding the different approaches academics have taken to writing about mindfulness practices in education. First, the authors highlight that studies were either conceptual or empirical and quantitative in nature. Rarely would studies straddle both conceptual and empirical approaches. Conceptual research looks at mindfulness from an origin-based perspective (Buddhism), whereas most empirical research seems to be focused on the psychological dimensions of mindfulness with a trend towards secularisation.

Second, Ergas and Hadar (2019) identified three roles mindfulness adopts in education: mindfulness *in* education, mindfulness *as* education, and mindfulness *of* education. These are shown in Table 2.1. Despite the differentiation the authors emphasise that all three patterns of mindfulness are grounded in the core facets: attention, intention, and attitude.

Mindfulness *in* education can include mindfulness-based interventions framed around wellbeing, physical and mental health to support student success, academic achievement and performance with a functional-economic

TABLE 2.1 The role of mindfulness in education (derived from Ergas and Hadar, 2019)

Elements	Mindfulness in education	Mindfulness as education	Mindfulness of education
Core facets of mindfulness	Attention, intention, attitude	Attention, intention, attitude	Attention, intention, attitude
Modalities of implementation	Socialisation-oriented mindfulness in education Mindfulness is a tool Mindfulness as therapy Mindfulness as economy Mindfulness made fit for the system Economic imperialism	Holistic mindfulness as education Mindfulness as a path To cultivate wisdom and compassion of (non)self.	Radical-critical mindfulness of education Contemplative inquiry First person perspective
Aims	Sustaining the system Solving problems of productivity, effectiveness, performance	Serve educational aims Liberation from suffering	Engaging in mindfulness for the purpose of critiquing education Inform critical thinking
Roles	Short-term interventions Secular, clinical, therapeutic, economic framings and language to fit the system	Focus on mindfulness activities rather than the outcome of the activity	Mindfulness of the breath, of the body to experience present moment in certain educational situations
Research	Quantitative	Conceptual/qualitative	Critical theory/pedagogy

goal in mind that suits the system it is applied to. For instance, if students feel high levels of stress and anxiety during assessment periods, mindfulness interventions are introduced to intervene with the experience in order to help students better prepare for the assessment and perform well. Similarly, mindfulness sessions might be offered to academics to reduce stress and burnout so they can continue teaching and meet performance goals. The aim of the mindfulness practice offered is to address a specific issue in the short term, it is system-based. Those participating learn to pay attention to the breath for instance and notice how it changes when feeling stressed. The intention is to learn to notice stress and focus on the sensations. Accepting the experience as it occurs is the attitude towards the present moment. Thus, the three core facets of mindfulness are still present.

In contrast, mindfulness *as* education builds upon the teachings of the Buddha, wisdom traditions and epistemology with a strong focus on self-knowledge and social inclusion. Publications tend to focus more on issues of integrating origin-based approaches in education such as reconceptualising learning and teaching practices, redesigning the curriculum, and adopting contemplative pedagogies aligned with experiential learning and inquiry-based ways of learning from using mindful language in the classroom to mindful assessment and feedback strategies. The authors found that mindfulness *as* education was more likely to be situated in social justice, attentive communication, negotiation classes as taught in business education, law and communications courses. Mindfulness practices still focus on attention, intention, and attitude as core facets but with the aim of establishing a long-term practice that functions as a path towards liberation from suffering. One might practise meditation every day for ten minutes, paying attention to the breath or other aspects, and set an intention for the day. Attitude towards what arises becomes a key ingredient in feeling at ease with the world as it unfolds.

Mindfulness *of* education is concerned with applying the concepts of introspection to the content of the experience. The experience itself becomes the object of observation and inquiry. The intention is to remain curious about what arises in the present moment. This might take a critical evaluation of the experience of assessment itself, for instance, how sitting an exam changes the quality of the breath, sensations of the body, and emotions and whether exam situations are of educational value.

This differentiation between roles of mindfulness in education is helpful to understand how to embed mindfulness in educational contexts. In my own experience it is often an amalgamation of *in, as,* and *of,* but I believe that it is more like an *and* relationship: mindfulness and business education. They are equal partners in the quest for developing self-aware and responsible future leaders. Mindfulness and business education form a unity; one cannot do without the other, or in Jon Kabbatt Zinn's words, shared by Ronald Purser (2019) in an article in the Guardian, 'The Mindfulness Conspiracy', 'mindfulness may actually be the only promise the species and the planet have for making it through the next couple of hundred years .'

2.2 VUCA and mindfulness – toughen up or soften down

With the above in mind, the question is what should we therefore teach in business schools? What matters for the future? Entrepreneurs, CEOs, and employers emphasise the need for business education to prepare students for a VUCA world: volatile, uncertain, complex and ambiguous. The term VUCA was coined by Bennis and Nanus (1985), although it was originally used by US Army as a response to the folding of the Union of Soviet Socialist Republics (USSR). In business education, the term VUCA is used to describe the environment of a business or political situation and how, if the circumstances of an event are volatile, uncertain, complex, and ambiguous, one needs to develop strategies to respond. However, the term has been overused to the point where VUCA just exists regardless. There is this notion that businesses operate in an unchangeable environment that will only get worse, and therefore graduates need to learn to toughen up in order successfully operate in such an environment. More often than not, we hear that the world of work is tough, ruthless, and unforgiving. It is a stream of negativity, and who would like to spend the rest of their life living in an environment that is destructive, soul-destroying, and bound to lead to unhappiness? If we continue to take that approach, how will the next generation lead us? Perhaps Donham anticipated the need for social responsibility to be part of business school teaching and culture, and we can only speculate on how our curriculum and graduates might act differently had it taken that turn. It is pointless to hypothesise the *what if* scenario, but one wonders. Despite the reality VUCA might describe, it is encouraging to find scholars who believe that there needs to be a different way and outlook we can share with graduates. A way that is truthful but also enjoyable, that can help develop skills. A way that is sustainable and has a positive impact on society.

Johansen and Euchner (2013) repurposed VUCA as vision, understanding, clarity, and agility and used these four characteristics to describe the *best* VUCA leader. Lawrence (2013) suggests Johansen's VUCA framework as a mechanism to design leadership programmes and develop leadership skills and abilities. Johansen's (2012) VUCA *Prime* framework acts like a response to Bennis and Nanus's (1985) VUCA term as shown in Table 2.2.

Operating in a volatile environment can be overwhelming for managers. Cognitive overload and feeling anxious and stressed leads to poor decision making. Volatility in life and in business means that something is severely out of balance, and how this something (e.g. prices, stock market, moods) will change is unpredictable; all that can be observed is that it changes quickly from one extreme to the next. It is like the goalposts are constantly moving, ultimately leaving the person trying to make a decision feel exhausted and unable to make informed decisions. To have the ability to keep the vision in sight, despite constant extreme change, requires the ability to centre oneself, focus, and concentrate. Such qualities and skills can be trained and are rooted in the four foundations of mindfulness.

Uncertainty, not knowing the outcome or not having sufficient knowledge or information to make good decisions as a leader requires the ability to pause, to observe, to listen, and to go within if needed. Pause, observe, and listen are strongly linked to the first foundation of mindfulness, mindfulness

TABLE 2.2 Comparison of VUCA frameworks

VUCA Bennis & Nanus (1985)	*VUCA Prime Johansen (2012)*
Volatile	Vision
Uncertain	Understanding
Complex	Clarity
Ambiguous	Agility

of the body, where one learns to observe the breath, listen to the breath, and take a moment to sit with the sensations in the body. From such practice comes insight, new ways of knowing, and new information. The situation that was once perceived as uncertain and threatening has most likely changed. It might be less threatening and endurable. Although, the situation might still be complex. Often complex situations do not have a simple straightforward solution, and the decision might involve a series of steps. Nason (2017) refers to this as a complexity mindset. In order to adopt such a complexity mindset, leaders need to develop the ability to zoom out and detach to gain clarity. Complexity is like clutter in the mind. The more we can declutter our mind, the easier it is to see through chaos objectively and rationally while staying aligned with body and mind, true to oneself. The second foundation of mindfulness, feeling tone provides individuals with a first step towards clarity by identifying thoughts, emotions, and situations as pleasant, unpleasant, or neutral. A clear mind allows us to notice fear for instance that might have blinded our ability to make decisions and our judgment. Instead of clinging to a set of data that might suggest one way to manage a particular situation, we might be able to draw in more data points and opinions. At the same time this trains our mind to become agile despite the ambiguity of a situation. The third foundation of mindfulness, mindfulness of the mind, trains our mind to know which thoughts and emotions lead to a specific outcome. The more we practice mindfulness of the mind, the more agile we become in making decisions and taking actions in a skilful manner that aids our role as leaders.

2.3 Mindfulness and leadership in business education

Given the focus of this book to develop future leaders by means of mindfulness approaches, it is important to briefly dive into leadership as a concept and how leadership entered business school research and teaching.

The study of leaders is probably as old as history itself. Leaders have existed since the emergence of civilisation and so does our interest in understanding who is a *good* leader and what makes that person a *good* leader. Leadership is a multi-disciplinary field of study in the social sciences, psychology, philosophy, anthropology, politics and business administration. Over the years, leadership positioned itself as a stand-alone subject in business. A clear definition of leadership, how to best measure leadership effectiveness, and its scope remain ongoing fodder for debate among leadership scholars. The debate has led to the development of many leadership approaches (Gutterman, 2023; Hunt & Fedynich, 2019; King, 1990), which are taught as standard globally in most higher education courses with business orientation. Table 2.3 provides a simplified and basic overview of the leadership periods, eras, and schools of thought most taught in business education. The beginning and end of an era or school of thought remains blurry at times, and in a way, leadership theories build on and extend one another.

TABLE 2.3 Leadership periods, eras, and school over time

Evolution eras of leadership (King, 1990)	Leadership schools of thought (Gutterman, 2023)	Leadership periods (Hunt and Fedynich, 2019)
Personality era *Great man, trait theory*	Trait school of leadership *Great man, Trait theory*	Second industrial revolution *Great man, trait theory*
Influence era *Power relations, persuasion*		Interregnum period *Power theory*
Behaviour era *Early behaviour – reinforced change theory, Ohio State & Michigan State studies* *Late behaviour theory – managerial grid, four factor theory, action theory, theory X and Y*	Behaviour school of leadership	Post-war years until 1980s *Behaviour* *Situation* *Contingency*
Situation era *Environment approach, open systems model, role attainment approach, leader role theory, sociotechnical systems*		
Contingency era *Contingency theory, path goal theory, multiple linkage model, normative theory*	Contingency school of leadership *Adoption of leadership styles*	
Transactional era *Exchange and social exchange theory*	Relational school of leadership *Leader–member exchange (LMX)*	
Anti-leadership era *Attribution approach, leadership substitute*	Information processing school of leadership	
Culture era *McKinsey 7-S, theory Z, self-leadership*		
Transformational era *Charisma, self-fulfilling prophecy*	New transformational leadership Contextual leadership	Leadership in the modern era *Transformational leadership* *Authentic leadership* *Servant leadership* *Follower-based leadership* *Evolutionary approach*

A strong focus remains on defining leadership, the quantitative nature of evaluating leadership effectiveness, and categorising leadership traits and styles by means of survey tools and scales to better understand who we are as leaders. Leadership is still also exclusively taught as disembodied, headship practice. Thus, teaching leadership seeks to explain leadership through obtaining data and interpreting it. It takes an external perspective and can only be understood as the study of (headship) leadership rather than obtaining qualities and skills that would serve the development of a whole-person approach, of *becoming* a leader (Sanyal & Rigg, 2021).

It is needless to say that understanding the history of leadership theory based on evaluation of how leaders and leadership evolved over time is fascinating and has allowed society to recognise the great and the not-so-great leaders. To acquaint students with the historical aspects of leadership, a typical exercise might be to ask students, at the beginning of a new leadership class, to name two leaders they believe are *great* leaders and two that they believe are less great. Usually, the discussion is dominated by an assessment of traits, qualities, behaviour, achievements, and successes of the individual in question. Similar to the various leadership theories and schools of thought the focus is on the individual's impact on the organisation, country, their followership. Even the traits that make the individual a *good* leader are discussed in the context of impact rather than in the context of the individual's relation to self. That aspect of leadership is more likely to fall under personal/professional development supported by coaching, which is less often taught or offered to undergraduate students in business schools. However, the underlying motivation for engaging in personal and professional development is not so much to become a great leader as to achieve the aim of getting a high-powered job in a reputable company that pays a decent salary. We do not ask students: 'Do you want to become a great leader? We ask: Where do you want to work? How much do you want to earn? What are your aspirations if you become team leader, managing director, partner, or CEO?

But leadership is not attached to a role per se. We lead ourselves every day, and the way we learned to lead ourselves determines how we lead others. Therefore, to develop skilful future leaders, business schools have to not just take responsibility but commit to providing an education that enables leadership skills development that goes beyond theorising about leadership and towards experiential learning of leadership. Such a commitment should be reflected in business school vision, mission, aims, and strategies.

Developing leadership skills might be included in employability programmes alongside team-working skills, communication skills, presentation skills, profile development to name a few. These services are usually offered centrally by university career and development departments and are geared towards meeting employer's needs. Students might even receive badges or a certificate that claims they have adopted certain employability skills, including leadership. There are a range of ways for students to demonstrate and reflect upon how they developed leadership skills, such as leading a project or leading the sports team. While experiential in nature, the acquisition of those skills are only recognised retrospectively. Learning takes place after, rather than in, the present moment and remains largely conceptual. Social entrepreneur, Sarah Harris in an interview with Plaskoff (2012) recommended 'learning by presence.' In her organisation, learning combines the heart and mind by utilising emotions and traditional business knowledge and skills to identify potential solutions to solve social needs. An assessment of how the body was perceived in a potential challenging situation, what emotions were felt, and how the mind operated in alignment is rarely included in such reflections. Yet these are the first data points we can use to inform our decision making. It is that level of self-awareness that underpins our actions, thoughts, and words. This process of connecting to self is required to develop leadership qualities that are aligned with one's values rather than with the values of an organisation. Thus, developing future leaders in business education must start as an experiential internal self-exploration journey at the very start of their business degree if not earlier.

2.4 Contemplative and embodied leadership

The marriage of leadership and mindfulness and its integration in business education is essential for the development of future leaders. Some might even say a *no brainer*. Krishnan (2021) emphasised that mindfulness is a critical skill for future leaders that can be learned over time through evidence-based and time-tested practice of mindfulness. Santorelli (2011) outlines that mindfulness practice helps cultivate the innate human qualities necessary for effective leadership and promotes self-actualisation that enables one to know oneself. Leadership infused with mindfulness enhances responsibility and accountability for our actions and actions we might take as a collective based on a shared vision.

Business leaders and entrepreneurs who have firmly integrated mindfulness as part of their organisational culture highlight that this marriage does not come without challenges though; it is perceived as a culture change that requires careful management and implementation. Most importantly the change needs to be supported by the executive board and reflected in a genuine commitment and investment aligned with a business school's vision and strategic goals. Introducing mindfulness into any organisation can only ever be an invitation.

A way of accelerating such culture change is to introduce different leadership approaches that feature the foundations of mindfulness and body–mind alignment. It is more essential than ever to teach contemplative leadership and embodied leadership in business schools, and it should probably be even more important than learning the historical development of leadership theory.

Contemplative leadership

Contemplative leadership is the element that is missing from the leadership approaches listed above, and it particularly aims at the awareness individuals need to develop as part of becoming leaders. Sims (2010) six suggestions to understand leadership are helpful to contextualise contemplative leadership:

Leadership is an activity, not an attribute.
Leadership is put together by several participants.
Leadership is done by the poet in residence.
Leadership is a contemplative art.
Leadership is a narrative art.
Leadership is a dialogic art.

It is surprising that Sims listed leadership as contemplative art fourth, because according to Sims' description of leadership as contemplative art and the need for a contemplative person, none of the other suggestions are possible without being contemplative. A contemplative person is aware of who they are. A contemplative person knows their qualities, knows their strengths and weaknesses, and most importantly, is grateful and content with this knowing. 'A contemplative person can be still, reflective, and *understand the world in quietness*' (Sims, 2010, p. 257). Sims' description refers to Walton's (1653) book *The Compleat Angler or the Contemplative Man's Recreation* (Walton & Cotton, 2014), but it also aligns with definitions and synonyms of the word contemplative found in most dictionaries: introspective, thoughtful, and meditative. A process where a person thinks about something carefully for a long time (Collins Dictionary, n. d.). However, Sims does not stop here. He continues to point out that contemplative leadership means to be at ease with the fact that people, including oneself as the leader, bring different skills and interest to a project. Furthermore, Sims emphasises that generosity plays a role in contemplative leadership and not just as an act of kindness towards the view of others with the aim of being liked and followed. It is more about acknowledging the significance of generosity in the context of leadership beyond one's own interests. Cultivating both awareness and generosity are at the heart of practicing mindfulness. Grandy and Sliwa (2017) take contemplative leadership definition a little further and propose contemplative leadership as 'virtuous activity; reflexive, engaged, relational, and embodied practice that requires knowledge from within context and practical wisdom' (p. 423). Embodied practice and practical wisdom are two additions that are equally important in the practice of mindfulness. The example given in relation to embodiment highlights the need to feel the connection to others participating in the virtuous activity. It is about supporting members of a team to find a rhythm together and sometimes this might mean helping them learn an instrument to tune in, to be aligned, while giving freedom to interpret, to move and make decisions based on their individual wisdom.

Embodied leadership

Hamill (2013) refers to embodied leadership as the somatic approach to developing leadership. Embodied leadership has often been positioned as relational leadership (Bathurst & Cain, 2013). Nathan (2021) describes embodied as the way to use body-based resources, which can help us to understand, make sense of, and derive meaning from a situation or an event and to link those insights to new ideas (future) and prior experiences (past). Fisher and Robbins (2015) beautifully explain that embodied leadership goes beyond the mind–body dichotomy and provides an acontextual approach to existing leadership theory then and now. We use our physical bodies to lead and through our physical actions, movement, and gestures (voluntarily and involuntarily) leadership is observed and judged. Sensations are a valuable source of information – bodily wisdom – to guide reactions and responses and contextualise circumstances. Embodied leadership is the interplay of body and mind aligned. In this process our thoughts, words, actions, sensations, and emotions dance together. They operate like an orchestra, which allows us to cultivate wisdom, to make decisions and lead others with the purpose of achieving a shared goal. Blake (2018) uses the term somatic intelligence to describe the alignment and explain how the interplay shapes the way we respond to ourselves and others. The body is a social and emotional sense organ, and we perceive the world through this lens. According to Blake (2018), three classes of embodied perception constitute this experience: exteroception, interoception, and proprioception. These ways of perceiving are also featured in the foundations of mindfulness and can be trained through regular practice. Exteroception includes our external senses: sight, sound, smell, taste, and touch. Interoception is the term used to describe internal visceral experience, which we know about through nerve cells of the heart, gut, lungs, skin, vagus nerve, and connective tissues. These cells give us information about our internal state. A person who is aware of these internal states responds differently to a person who is not (Blake, 2022). Proprioception refers to the sensory experience of balance and our knowing and experience of where our body is positioned in proximity to other people, objects, or noises. The inner ear, particular muscle cells, and connective tissue are crucial in that process.

The way to train these ways of perceiving and utilising somatic intelligence effectively as a leader requires self-awareness training, which mindfulness practice can offer. Fogel (2013) distinguishes between conceptual and embodied self-awareness. Conceptual self-awareness is factual information about oneself (e.g. birth date, school names, personal experiences in past and future scenarios underpinned by insights, values, desires). Eurich (2018) divides the concept of self-awareness further into internal and external self-awareness, beyond just knowing personal qualities. Internal self-awareness looks at understanding oneself from the inside. This internal perspective enables us to see ourselves clearly by knowing and understanding our values, passions, aspirations, behaviour, and impact on others. In contrast, external self-awareness is about understanding oneself from the outside, being able to take an outsider perspective towards oneself and how others might perceive one. Too much internal or too much external self-awareness creates an imbalance. Developing embodied self-awareness through the experience of sensing, feeling, and acting in the present moment can be a great tool to equalise such discrepancy. Embodied self-awareness might include noticing changes in body temperature, exploring pain, observing the breath, energy levels, moods and emotions arising. For me, embodied self-awareness is the pinnacle of leadership. Without awareness intelligence, we are unable to have somatic or emotional experiences. Yet we rarely learn or are taught at home, at school, or later, at university and work how to access our innate awareness intelligence and how to use it effectively to foster relationships at work and at home and to lead with body, mind, and heart.

Chapter 2 in a nutshell...

Mindfulness and business education must be equal partners, a marriage built on a common intention to make the world a better place for future generations. This is an intention that has been there since the beginning, since the birth of business schools. We can understand this marriage as a vehicle to navigate the volatile, uncertain, complex, and ambiguous waters businesses are faced with.

It is time to instil a new way of knowing, thinking, and doing business education by means of experiential teaching and learning of mindfulness, contemplative and embodied leadership, and awareness intelligence in alignment with standard business subjects (e.g. finance, strategy, marketing, operations, people management) and contemporary challenges and opportunities faced by businesses and society. In a nutshell, business schools should incorporate and teach:

1. Mindfulness: foundations of mindfulness, mindfulness practice including yoga, meditation, coaching and journaling.
2. Leadership: contemplative and embodied leadership theory and practice.
3. Awareness intelligence: Somatic and emotional intelligence, self-awareness.

References

Acton, R. M. (2023). The search for social harmony at Harvard Business School, 1919–1942. *Modern Intellectual History*, 20(1), 141–167.
Bathurst, R., & Cain, T. (2013). Embodied leadership: The aesthetics of gesture. *Leadership*, 9(3), 358–377.
Bennis, W., & Nanus, B. (1985). *Leaders: Strategies for taking charge*. Harper & Row.

Bennis, W. G., & O'Toole, J. (2005). How business schools have lost their way. *Harvard Business Review*, 83(5), 96–104.

Blake, A. (2018). *Your body is your brain: Leverage your somatic intelligence to find purpose, build resilience, deepen relationships and lead more powerfully*. Trokay Press.

Blake, A. (2022). *Embodied awareness, embodied practice: A powerful path to practical wisdom*. Case Western Reserve University.

Bruce, K., & Nyland, C. (2011). Elton Mayo and the deification of human relations. *Organization Studies*, 32(3), 383–405.

Bryant, S. M., Cullen, P. G., & Iannarelli, J. E. (2022). A vison for management education: The AACSB perspective. In M. Fellenz, S. Hoidn, & M. Brady (Eds.) *The future of management education* (pp.225–243). Routledge.

Collins Dictionary. (n.d.). Contemplative. In *CollinsDictionary.com*. Retrieved July 25, 2024, from https://www.collinsdictionary.com/#google_vignette.

Ergas, O., & Hadar, L. L. (2019). Mindfulness in and as education: A map of a developing academic discourse from 2002 to 2017. *Review of Education*, 7(3), 40.

Eurich, T. (2018). What self-awareness really is (and how to cultivate it). *Harvard Business Review*, 4, 2–8.

Fisher, K., & Robbins, C. R. (2015). Embodied leadership: Moving from leader competencies to leaderful practices. *Leadership*, 11(3), 281–299.

Fogel, A. (2013). *The psychophysiology of self-awareness: Rediscovering the lost art of body sense*. WW Norton & Company.

Grandy, G., & Sliwa, M. (2017). Contemplative leadership: The possibilities for the ethics of leadership theory and practice. *Journal of Business Ethics*, 143, 423–440.

Gutterman, A. (2023). *History and evolution of leadership*. SSRN. http://dx.doi.org/10.2139/ssrn.4552091.

Hamill, P. (2013). *Embodied leadership: The somatic approach to developing your leadership*. Kogan Page Publishers.

Hunt, T., & Fedynich, L. (2019). Leadership: Past, present, and future: An evolution of an idea. *Journal of Arts and Humanities*, 8(2), 22–26.

Johansen, B., & Euchner, J. (2013). Navigating the VUCA world. *Research-Technology Management*, 56(1), 10–15.

Johansen, R. (2012). *Leaders make the future: Ten new leadership skills for an uncertain world*. Berrett-Koehler Publishers.

King, A. S. (1990). Evolution of leadership theory. *Vikalpa*, 15(2), 43–56.

King, W. R., Premkumar, G., & Ramamurthy, K. (1990). An evaluation of the role and performance of a decision support system in business education. *Decision Sciences*, 21(3), 642–659.

Krishnan, H. A. (2021). Mindfulness as a strategy for sustainable competitive advantage. *Business Horizons*, 64(5), 697–709.

Lawrence, K. (2013). *Developing leaders in a VUCA environment*. UNC Kenan-Flagler Business School, https://www.emergingrnleader.com/wp-content/uploads/2013/02/developing-leaders-in-a-vuca-environment.pdf.

Locke, E. A. (1982). The ideas of Frederick W. Taylor: An evaluation. *Academy of Management Review*, 7(1), 14–24.

Nason, R. (2017). *It's not complicated: The art and science of complexity in business*. University of Toronto Press.

Nathan, M. J. (2021). *Foundations of embodied learning: A paradigm for education*. Routledge.

Plaskoff, J. (2012). Building the heart and the mind: An interview with leading social entrepreneur Sarah Harris. *Academy of Management Learning & Education*, 11(3), 432–441.

Purser, R. (2019). The mindfulness conspiracy. *The Guardian*. https://www.theguardian.com/lifeandstyle/2019/jun/14/the-mindfulness-conspiracy-capitalist-spirituality.

Santorelli, S. F. (2011). 'Enjoy your death': Leadership lessons forged in the crucible of organizational death and rebirth infused with mindfulness and mastery. *Contemporary Buddhism*, 12(1), 199–217.

Sanyal, C., & Rigg, C. (2021). Integrating mindfulness into leadership development. *Journal of Management Education*, 45(2), 243–264.

Sims, D. (2010). Looking for the key to leadership under the lamp post. *European Management Journal*, 28(4), 253–259.

Spender, J. C. (2017). *A brief and non-academic history of management education*. AACSB. https://www.aacsb.edu/insights/articles/2017/03/brief-non-academic-history-management-education.

Walton, I., & Cotton, C. (2014). *The compleat angler*. OUP Oxford.

Wren, D. A., & Van Fleet, D. D. (1983). History in schools of business. *Business and Economic History*, 12, 29–35.

Zeff, S. A. (2008). The contribution of the Harvard Business School to management control, 1908–1980. *Journal of Management Accounting Research*, 20(s1), 175–208.

PART II
What to consider in the marriage of mindfulness and business education

3
PURPOSE, MEASURING, AND PEDAGOGY

Over the last ten years, studies concerned with integrating mindfulness into learning and teaching in business education have risen. Most emphasise the positive impact of integrating mindfulness practices in the classroom and outside the classroom and the benefits to student wellbeing, performance, and success. Some initiatives have been rooted in Buddhist psychology and philosophy whereas others have taken a more secular approach. Most mindfulness initiatives were trialled once or twice and remain singular events but there is also evidence of semester-long initiatives and ways of measuring students' disposition to mindfulness. However, such studies, concerned with introducing and embedding mindfulness practices in business education, heavily rely upon academics who already have a positive relationship with mindfulness and are passionate about sharing their own practice with the purpose of supporting student and staff development (Ergas & Hadar, 2019).

Scholars such as Joan F. Marques who wrote *The Awakened Leader* (2007), Tom Elwood Culham (2013), or Sophia Town et al. (2024) have contributed greatly to our understanding of mindfulness practices in the management classroom and beyond. The roots of most scholars lead back to leadership, business ethics and organisational behaviour studies. However, we can also find scholars in subjects that are less obviously concerned with integrating mindfulness into the classroom, such as accounting and finance, economics, sustainability, and more recently, artificial intelligence. Thus, the integration of mindfulness practices into business education is applicable and open to all business school departments.

Mindfulness initiatives have been introduced at both undergraduate and postgraduate level in business schools and feature in many areas such as ethical decision making, leadership, organisational behaviour to name a few (Burton et al., 2021; McGhee & Grant, 2015; Roberts, 2021; Sadler-Smith &

DOI: 10.4324/9781032637464-6

Shefy, 2007; Vu & Burton, 2020). Other areas where mindfulness has been successfully used are to support regulation of emotions, stress management, engagement, and anxiety (Chiang & Sumell, 2019; Harajli & Norré, 2023) in both organisational and educational contexts. However, there are also examples of introducing mindfulness concepts to subjects such as economics accounting and finance to encourage openness and receptivity to concepts often perceived as dull (Borker, 2013; Kuechler & Stedham, 2018).

The question is what difference do we want our students, leaders of the future, to make in organisations and society? Do we want to foster ethical mindset development, equip future leaders with mindfulness skills to be more resilient, or simply to create a space for students to become reflective and reflexive, open to new perspectives? Our intention as business educators is pivotal in determining the place mindfulness might have in business education in the future. What would you like your students to take away and remember when they graduate? What sort of leader would you like to see in the future and what impact do you want your students to have in the world?

3.1 Purpose of mindfulness and business education

Encouraging openness and ethical decision making

Hooman's wrote in *Leading Edge* in March 2015 (Hoomans, 2015) that the average American adult makes 35,000 decisions a day. It is a complicated mental and unconscious process even though we might believe that all our decisions are the result of a rational and conscious operation. (Kahneman, 2011) refers to two modes of thinking which are widely understood in psychology: thinking fast and thinking slow. Thinking fast is called system 1 thinking, and thinking slow is referred to as system 2 thinking. System 1 thinking happens ad hoc, automatically, unconsciously, and outside our control. System 2, in contrast, is described as the conscious approach that is based on reason and taking time where thoughts are created step by step. Both systems are necessary and have their place in our day-to-day. Kahneman (2011) gives a series of examples for system 1 thinking, such as: complete the phrase 'bread and ...', 2 + 2 = ? or reading words on large billboards while driving. System 2 thinking is designed to help us make more difficult and challenging decisions, which require consideration of multiple aspects and are affected by the external world, such as making decisions in a VUCA environment.

Our decisions are also influenced by our own beliefs, values, memories, and the emotions we experience in any given situation. Therefore, decision making can be biased by emotions and result in unethical behaviour intentionally and unintentionally. In the literature such behaviour is described as having *ethical blind spots* (Sezer et al., 2015). However, mindfulness practice can develop one's awareness so that one can identify ethical blind spots (Lampe & Engleman-Lampe, 2012) so as to move from system 1 to system 2 thinking and to learn to make decisions that reflect rationality and intuition (Sadler-Smith and Shefy, 2007). Harajli and Norré (2023) emphasise that the purpose of business education is not just to teach students about ethical decision making from an intellectual perspective but to ensure that business students develop the ability to make ethical decisions. Incorporating mindfulness practice into the curriculum enhances students' acceptance of new perspectives (Kuechler and Stedham, 2018) such as increased ethical behaviour (McGhee and Grant, 2015). Burton et al. (2021) used mindful reflexivity to enable students to identify responsible business practices. This included the evaluation of their own actions as leaders in the context of making responsible and ethical decisions. Students are invited to share an ethical dilemma they have personally experienced or witnessed in some way. The authors use three elements of mindful reflexivity rooted in Buddhist concepts: impermanence, dependent arising, and nonself. Students are asked a number of questions in relation to those elements and explore their past experience, motives, involvement, and actions. After individually reflecting upon the ethical dilemma experience, students are invited to discuss their insights and the implications of their learning in their working environment. Alongside, students are encouraged to journal and write down their feelings and thoughts in regard to the ethical dilemmas they discussed. Thus, ethical decision making requires students to learn and practice self-reflexivity (Hibbert & Cunliffe, 2015), which mindfulness approaches can support.

Being able to make ethical decisions is a helpful skill for future leaders, but it requires openness to new perspectives. Cultivating an openness to something new implicitly increases a certain readiness for learning, but the questions is how can students be supported to become more open? Mindfulness concepts have provided business educators with ideas not just to transmit technical knowledge about ethical approaches in accounting and finance but to instil an openness and appreciation for ethical behaviour at a personal level. Borker (2013) emphasises specifically the need for business educators in accounting and finance to find ways of engaging students in ethical discourse to foster openness and spark curiosity. The rise of financial scandals and fraudulent behaviour in the industry provides fertile ground to practise such behaviour and engage students in different ways of learning. Thus, the benefits of mindfulness approaches in accounting education go beyond developing an ethical mindset related to managerial accounting and finance practice. To encourage openness, Borker (2013) explains that class should start with a short mindfulness practice, which invites students to take an active part in learning rather than remaining passive. This short mindfulness session at the beginning is used as a gateway to cultivating openness to the topic discussed that week for instance. By focusing the emphasis on openness and receiving information, the author found that students, despite perceiving the subject matter as boring and dry, were able to engage in class.

Utilising an active learning approach with experiential elements is not new in management education. (Reynolds & Vince, 2007). Active learning refers to educators and students creating, sharing and reflecting upon knowledge together. There are many active learning strategies educators have adopted in business education for online and offline learning and teaching including flipped classroom and experiential learning techniques (Rivers, 2021; Robertson, 2018) which can all feature aspects of mindfulness. The use of mindfulness practices in the classroom is understood as experiential learning (Burton et al., 2021).

It is fair to say that despite efforts to incorporate experiential learning in the classroom, keeping students engaged remains a challenge. Students are easily distracted by technology during class, which results in students being physically present but mentally absent from learning and the space around them. There are two ways to address this issue. First, invite students to measure their own engagement through mindfulness scales and/or, second, draw students attention to the science of distracted mind states and their impact on performance, decision making, and sustaining relationships (Gazzaley and Rosen, 2016). An MBA student who was attending one of my five-week mindfulness programmes, 'Know yourself,' said to me during the third workshop, which focused on mindfulness of the mind: *I cannot believe I am saying this, but I think I am addicted to distraction. My mind is always distracted, I seek distraction.* What the MBA student described is not unusual. Gazzaley and Rosen (2016) use the term *information-seeking creatures* to describe our endless hunger for seeking information. So, no wonder it is challenging for educators to keep students engaged and focused. Technology expedites retrieval of information, which results in instant gratification of our perpetual need to seek, which in turn opens new avenues for perceiving and understanding the world around us and yet further need for information.

Enhancing emotional intelligence

Throughout engaging in self-reflexive practices infused by mindfulness concepts, the exploration of emotions and how these impact our thoughts and actions is inevitable. Yet, in business education the predominant approach to learning is governed by intellect-oriented learning and teaching approaches instead of emotionally grounded pedagogies (Burton et al., 2021). In particular, the consideration of emotions in making decisions has often been alluded to as poor decision making, as discussed previously. Separating emotions from thoughts, though, is an almost inhuman task because emotions are central to our human experience. Learning and understanding how emotions arise and how to interpret them without attaching is crucial to regulating emotions and making effective and ethical decisions. The key is to learn to regulate emotions and use emotions effectively, intentionally, and intelligently. Mindfulness practices provide the opportunity to experiment and to develop self-awareness, self-regulation, social skills, empathy, and motivation, which are the five components of emotional intelligence. Emotionally grounded pedagogies create a space for students to work with their emotions, individually and collectively through peer learning. It is widely understood that developing emotional intelligence requires deep personal internal work and practising such skills can be perceived as unusual in a business school context.

Meditation has been found to support such inner work (Burton et al., 2021), as a tool to observe the internal experience. At first students might feel uncomfortable practicing ten-minute meditations at the beginning of class, but after a couple of times, the practice is normalised. Burton and colleagues (2021) highlight the importance of giving management students space after meditation to share their experience in small constellations such as pairs or triads and encouraging journaling to document their development journey. It is through those conversations and reflective writing events that students can learn about each other's emotional experiences. While journals might not be graded, embedding the overall experiences of the intervention and journey in a summative assessment component can be a powerful way for students and educators to assess the transformational quality of the intervention and inner work.

Harajli and Norré (2023) shared their experiences of using a mood meter exercise at the beginning and end of class to enable management students to tap into their emotional intelligence. The study was conducted in a business school in Lebanon in 2019, at a time of political, social, and economic turmoil. The authors explained that they played classical music while students answered a couple of questions about their state of being: How are you feeling today? What are your emotions today? What is your level of energy? In addition to using the mood metre students were invited to join a short meditation. The exercise was very well perceived by students who expressed their gratitude to the teacher and shared their transformational journeys in heartwarming statements submitted as part of their student evaluations. The statements outlined the positive impact of mindfulness practices on their personal wellbeing and ability to cope with external challenges. Students reported increased self-awareness and the ability to manage emotions better in times of distress.

The insights shared above have also been reported by Taylor and Bishop (2019) who offered mindfulness as a tool to reclaim self-awareness of management students in undergraduate and graduate leadership courses. Mindfulness was positioned as a cornerstone of personal leadership practice. Students were encouraged to engage in a variety of mindfulness practices, starting by creating space for mindful activities in class and outside class. These included journaling, spending time in nature, and visualising opportunities for development and growth. Research on the benefits of mindfulness was shared with the students, including how mindfulness approaches can increase the performance and productivity of employees and organisations as a whole. The authors used the Mindful Attention Awareness Scale (MAAS) and the Kentucky Inventory of Mindfulness Skills (Baer et al., 2006) scale to measure the how students' perception of mindfulness changed throughout the course. Evaluation of personal reflections revealed that students felt more focused, calm and that their ability to regulate emotions improved.

3.2 Measuring effectiveness of mindfulness in business school classroom

Active engagement plays a crucial role in promoting wellbeing and transformative learning (Bowden et al., 2021). Chiang and Sumell (2019) conducted a study that asked: Are your students absent, not absent, or present? The authors were interested in understanding the frequency with which mobile devices were used during teaching as a measure of classroom mindfulness. The premise is that to be mindful a person is required to be present and focused while abstaining from external distractions. While the study did not introduce a mindfulness practice per se, measuring dispositional mindfulness levels in the classroom and sharing insights with students might help students to become aware of their relationship with self, noticing when they are being present and when they are distracted. The authors used MAAS to measure this relationship. MAAS measures an individual's awareness in the present moment in everyday tasks (Brown & Ryan, 2003). Students were asked to evaluate statements according to three mindfulness environments. These were complemented by three mindfulness index variables as shown in Table 3.1.

Chiang and Sumell's (2019) study showed a strong positive association between mindfulness and student performance. While the authors acknowledge that the findings were not able to confirm whether higher mindfulness levels would improve performance, higher dispositional mindfulness levels, less mobile usage, and reduced exam anxiety levels have been found to affect student performance positively. So perhaps we should prohibit mobile phones in the classroom. Such a behaviour change might also address the rising student engagement issues business schools are facing (Bowden et al., 2021) and promote ongoing active engagement as outlined above. On the other hand, a less radical approach might be to share insights of such research with students. The question business students often ask is *how can I perform really well, what do I need to do?* Students can be given the choice of turning their mobile phone off at the beginning of class. In addition, this process could be accompanied by an invitation to join a short mindfulness meditation to indicate their commitment and set an intention to be active and present. Such

TABLE 3.1 Mindfulness environments and indexes adopted from Chiang and Sumell (2019)

Mindfulness environments	*Mindfulness index variables*
General dispositional mindfulness	MAAS index
Classroom mindfulness	Mobile index (mobile device usage)
Assessment mindfulness	Anxiety index (levels of exam anxiety)

approaches can have a ritual-like feel and support students in settling into the active learning space. We will revisit suggestions like that in more depth in the *How* part. However, the positive impact of mindfulness on students' performance, and particularly business analysis and decision making, has been studied in depth by Asthana (2021), a researcher from Peru. Their research showed that mindfulness reduced stress and led to higher levels of proficiency in making decisions. MAAS was used to explore the relationship between mindfulness, stress, and higher levels of proficiency. The findings confirmed that one third of the positive impact on higher levels of proficiency in decision making was related to reduced stress and two thirds to mindfulness practice. In another study conducted by the author, MAAS was used to measure the impact of yoga practices on academic performance and what role mindfulness plays in this context. The study demonstrated that mindfulness increases prosocial behaviour and acts as a mediator between yoga practices and academic performance (Asthana, 2023). MAAS appears to be a helpful tool in assessing student awareness and identifying the impact of mindfulness initiatives or practices on management students.

Kay and Young (2022) conducted a quasi-experimental study to measure the positive effect of two months of online mindfulness training on cultivating authenticity among 227 postgraduate management students. Data was collected by means of Five Facets Mindfulness Questionnaires (FFMQ), which is one of eight well known scales, along with MAAS, to measure mindfulness aspects (Baer et al., 2006). Quantitative findings confirmed that students who engaged in online mindfulness training felt an increase in psychological wellbeing. Furthermore, students who scored high on conscientiousness were able to cultivate their authentic sense of self, which was reported as greater self-awareness. (Schultz & Ryan, 2015) emphasise that students who have a more advanced sense of mindfulness are more likely to act reflectively, considerately, and authentically. The benefits of acting authentically and becoming an authentic leader are often highlighted by business educators as a *good to develop trait*. According to Kay and Young (2022), support for students to learn and cultivate authenticity is scarce in business schools but the authors advocate mindfulness training as a mechanism to foster the connection to self and ultimately develop an authentic self. An authentic leader is someone who acts in accordance with their values and beliefs, to stay true to themselves, know themselves, which requires internal and external self-awareness (Eurich, 2017).

These insights help us to understand that online mindfulness training can have greater benefits for students who are already conscientious and can improve psychological wellbeing. This insight ties in well with the description of a *good* leader because conscientiousness is one of the big five personality traits (Northouse, 2021). A conscientious person is often described as someone who is organised, reliable, and able to regulate emotions well. The challenge of the latter though is the reason why mindfulness has found its way into organisations and receives attention in business education now. Stress and pressure whether at work or through studying can have a negative impact on managing emotions, which in turn can cloud judgment and the ability to make ethical decisions.

3.3 Facilitation: Skills, knowledge, and ethics

The above examples indicate a positive impact of introducing and facilitating mindfulness concepts and practices in business education. It is easy to just pay attention to the benefits. However, some studies reported a mixed response to the introduction of mindfulness activities in the classroom. Sadler-Smith and Shefy (2007) utilised mindfulness to introduce the concept of intuition in management. The project aimed to support MBA students in developing intuitive awareness, which would serve them in working life as managers. The programme was designed to engage students in direct experiences and for them, through that awareness, to learn about their own intuitive processes and how these impact their behaviour and decision making as managers. The programme offered both in-class and out-side class activities. The authors developed ten activities students could choose from and asked them to rank them in preference. The three most preferred activities were mindful exercises that involved drawing, spontaneous writing, and sitting meditation. The least preferred activities were love and kindness exercises and visual and walking meditations. Responses from the students showed that some enjoyed learning these techniques and shared that they would use them to focus and calm down but not in a working environment. Love and kindness exercises made students feel too self-conscious. They felt it was removed from the world they knew. It was experienced as too weird. Although the study took place in 2007, and mindfulness has since received a lot of attention within and outside management education, these experiences are not uncommon, and the advice given by Sadler-Smith and Shefy (2007, p. 200) for how to design programmes is invaluable:

> *Exercises need to be simple (not too many steps), practical (readily carried out in home or workplace environments), and credible (not seen as too far-out or weird) ... the adoption of the majority of these techniques into typical MBA programs is likely to be unproblematic when prototyped and facilitated competently.*

What competencies and skills would business educators need to design effective programmes?

Hadar and Ergas (2022) emphasise that those who teach mindfulness should have knowledge and appreciation for its roots and historical development. It is not hard to read about mindfulness techniques and find scripts online to support such teachings. However, facilitation of such sessions goes beyond transmission of knowledge and a purely intellectual approach. Burton et al. (2021) call for a shift from intellect-oriented pedagogies to emotionally grounded pedagogies that are experiential in nature. In fact, I would add that mindfulness sessions include the development of the intellectual and emotional experiences of participants. Thus, educators need to be prepared and have the necessary knowledge and skills to support students on their experiential journey of becoming physically, mentally, and emotionally grounded individuals who can apply their insights as leaders in the future.

How one obtains specific knowledge and skills and continues to develop one's own practice is an important question to consider. On the one hand, business educators need to have knowledge of mindfulness itself, pedagogic approaches to underpin their teachings, and self-knowledge. Let us start with self-knowledge. The question that arises is what makes someone want to introduce and teach mindfulness to management students? Harajli and Norré (2023) explain that their motivations and reasons for teaching mindfulness are grounded in their own practice. At the beginning of a new class, the authors would share with students their educational and professional journey and also their interests and passions. One of the authors highlights a long-term love of meditation. Sadler-Smith and Shefy (2007) also indicate a dedication to and fascination with mindfulness. I followed up with Eugene Sadler-Smith, who happens to be a good colleague, and I asked him about his article. I discovered that mindfulness was Shefy's metier, whereas Sadler-Smith enjoyed merging the concepts of intuition and mindfulness and learning about it theoretically.

Personal references about one's relationship with mindfulness are rare in academic publications, and one can only assume that authors have their own practice or some relationship to mindfulness that drives them to introduce and teach. I am often asked if it is necessary for someone who wants to introduce and teach mindfulness to have an established self-practice. I would say it is preferable if mindfulness is introduced and taught experientially beyond knowledge transmission. Personal experience is at the forefront of any mindfulness tool one might want to introduce and use. For instance, walking meditation has been perceived by management students as the least favourable (Sadler-Smith and Shefy, 2007), whereas Gelles (2015) found that employees enjoyed walking meditation as a means to break up their working day. In my own workshops, I use walking meditation. Some participants find it makes them feel restless, and others experience it as a new way of connecting to themselves. One of the participants in a recent course said it feels like learning to walk again. My own experience with walking meditation was challenging too. I had to learn it and become comfortable with the slow movement and comfortable with others not enjoying it and voicing their discomfort. However, without my own experience, I would not have been able to empathise with such experiences, and I would not have been able to speak to potential experiences while facilitating walking meditation. The ability to speak to people's experiences is crucial, and therefore I believe that self-practice is needed. Only if those facilitating such sessions can speak to different experiences, are participants able to develop their own awareness of it, whether it is appreciation or rejection. In addition, speaking to one's experiences validates their experiences, which is equally important in such settings. At times participants worry that *they are doing it wrong*, yet there is very little to do wrong, there are only different experiences. The extent of self-practice is individual of course. It might be daily; it might a couple of times throughout the week. However, the more we practice the more comfortable we become and the more confident we are sharing practice, knowledge, and insight with others. I would not have felt comfortable teaching mindfulness without self-practice and continuous professional development. Similarly, I would feel very uncomfortable teaching a subject I am not familiar with.

How one starts one's mindfulness journey and establishes a regular and effective self-practice is a personal endeavour. Since mindfulness has risen in popularity, so have opportunities for obtaining qualifications to enhance practice and teaching. The choice of qualification depends upon whether one would like to take an experiential or intellect-based teaching approach and whether one would like to develop teaching skills. Master courses in mindfulness based cognitive therapy offer a different foundation for teaching mindfulness than conventional yoga and meditation teacher training courses that are rooted in the principles of mindfulness. Both explore the foundations of mindfulness, but they are probably at opposite ends of a spectrum. While most MBCT (mindfulness based cognitive therapy) and MBSR (mindfulness based stress reduction) courses have a self-practice element as a requirement, yoga and meditation teacher training courses expect students to already have an established self-practice, and the majority of learning is on mindfulness in practice and application. In my own experience, colleagues have obtained a mixture of qualifications and continue to do so even though they have already been teaching for many years. My gateway into mindfulness teaching was supported by an executive coaching qualification (Academy of Executive Coaching), meditation teacher training (British School of Meditation), and various yoga teacher training courses with House of Yoga. I commit to engage in at least one professional development opportunity each year, from courses on a specific aspect related to mindfulness, yoga, meditation, or coaching to going on a retreat. Alongside this, I widen my knowledge with seminars, readings, and dissemination. This approach works well for me and the way I want to introduce and teach mindfulness in business education and beyond. Thus, finding the right path depends on personal circumstances, time, funds, and objectives.

Embarking upon a qualification in mindfulness teaching is more than just gaining credentials and a certificate. Every course and retreat I have attended and completed has expanded my network. The connections I have made and the experiences we all shared allowed us to bond and draw on each other and collaborate. While business schools are slowly recognising the benefit of introducing mindfulness in the curriculum, mindfulness academics are still in the minority, not just in business schools but in higher education institutions too. This also means that obtaining such qualifications might require private investment. However, with a good business case in hand and a strategy, the continuous professional development pot might consider making a contribution. It is worth identifying the benefits and setting out such a strategy for the school. I submitted a proposal for coaching colleagues in the school and offering free meditations to all university students throughout term to address work or assessment stress and anxiety. For these purposes, my institution funded my coaching and meditation teacher training course. Most of my other qualifications were privately funded.

Regardless of the qualification, it is paramount to keep in mind that teaching mindfulness does not replace clinical services. It is a misconception to believe that mindfulness replaces the need for wellbeing services or therapy. As part of any qualification, teachers and coaches are governed by a code of conduct and code of ethics. Codes of conduct and codes of ethics outline clearly that mindfulness teachers are neither mental health practitioners nor therapists. Therefore, a qualification can also be a good gateway to setting boundaries and offering ethical and responsible learning and teaching facilitation.

A good teacher training programme will address ethical and operational challenges and provide tools to manage these effectively. Especially if teaching is taking place experientially, it is common for participants to be affected in one way or another. Such experiences might express themselves in feeling upset, tears and laughter, or the need to go for a walk. Being able to deal with these experiences and giving space is a skill. The purpose of a mindfulness teacher is to guide and enable participants to explore their connection to self in the present moment and to become comfortable in using various tools to manage and regulate emotions, thoughts, and sensations as they arise. The purpose is not to explore the past or set out a coping strategy. This would be the remit of a therapist. Mindfulness teachers and coaches work on the principle of guidance: all our answers are within us, and we ourselves are the best teachers. Learning takes place through experience of observing thoughts, emotions, and sensations. Therefore, classrooms become experiential learning spaces.

Dean et al. (2020) strongly emphasise that educators who adopt an experiential pedagogy in the classroom must have specific skills beyond classical didactic ways of teaching. The authors specifically focus on the fact that the outcome of experiential activities does not end when class finishes. Instead, the impact might be longer lasting than educators have anticipated and might leave students feeling distressed, angry, or anxious, or it might even alter relationships between students or between students and educators. Thus, the ability to manage outcomes skilfully becomes even more relevant. As mentioned above, being able to speak to potential emotional and behavioural outcomes is one way to reassure students and mitigate the risk of unplanned responses. Another suggestion would be to risk-assess mindfulness activities and incorporate information about risks as part of the debrief. A combination of the two might be preferable. In addition, I would suggest incorporating sufficient space and breaks for students throughout experiential mindfulness practices to reflect and use their inner wisdom to respond to their experience. Because awareness and regulation of emotions is at the heart of mindfulness practices, it is fair to say that managing unplanned responses becomes slightly easier compared to experiential activities in management classes that focus not on awareness but on *testing* students in a way that provokes behaviour and divergent thinking, such as Jane Elliott's blue-eyed, brown-eyed exercise (Bloom, 2022). A video of the experiment can be found on YouTube with the title 'Jane Elliott's Brown Eye/Blue Eye Test ' (University of Northern Iowa, 2020).

3.4 Educational concepts for mindfulness and business education

Experiential learning might be a suitable and accepted way to introduce and teach mindfulness theoretically and practically. Other pedagogies that are associated with teaching mindfulness are contemplative pedagogy, pedagogy of care/self-care, and more recently, a new term has arisen, pedagogy for humanised leadership. The latter emphasises the connection between mindfulness and leadership and its need for introduction and incorporation into business education.

Contemplative pedagogy is the most prominent learning and teaching approach associated with mindfulness. It usually refers to learning how to cultivate emotional balance, concentration, attention, and focus. Developing altruistic behaviours and compassion are other educational goals of contemplative pedagogy (Zajonc, 2013). Over the years, several contemplative pedagogy centres have emerged in higher education, and these offer training as well as conducting research on the benefits of contemplative pedagogy for learning, teaching, and personal development. Most centres are nestled within well-established learning and teaching centres (e.g. University of Massachusetts Amherts, Vanderbilt University, Montclair State University), with minor exceptions, such as Stanford University's (Doty, 2016) Center for Compassion and Altruism Research and Education or the Centre for Excellence in Mindfulness Research at City University, London, United Kingdom. Thus, contemplative pedagogy and business education are not naturally matched unless in the context of teaching ethics in business schools (Culham, 2013). As touched upon in Part 1, the term *contemplative* is more likely to be introduced in relation to the concept of contemplative leadership.

Another pedagogy that I believe is worthwhile adding is *pedagogy of care*. Socrates referred to education as caring, in the sense of caring for the young and giving them the best opportunities to grow into wise and kind beings who understand to care for themselves and others. It is our responsibility to support students on their way of developing an inner desire to care about themselves and others through learning (Mortari, 2016). This requires a path that enables them to develop the necessary cognitive skills, behaviours, and attitudes needed to cultivate the need and desire for self-care and care of others. Through this process, students are likely to find meaning in their existence. This does not mean that business students should pursue charitable careers, but it does mean that business educators need to embed mechanisms and content that allows students to critically evaluate the impact of certain decisions and behaviours on the welfare of others. Ethics and sustainability are great avenues to cultivate a sense of care and caring. Mindfulness allows students to take it to the next level and question the impact of their decision making on others and themselves and evaluate the degree of mindful thinking and acting required to foster a culture of caring around them from small assessment groups or part-time work to social engagements. Mortari (2016) outlines two important concepts: receptiveness and responsiveness. Receptiveness refers to the openness of an educator to accepting that students have different experiences, especially in the context of mindfulness teaching. Responsiveness is concerned with the educator's cognitive and emotional ability to manage such differences in the classroom in an inclusive and empathetic manner. It is the educator's duty to model receptiveness and responsiveness in a way that has a positive impact on student behaviour and attitudes. Mortari (2016) goes on to highlight eight relational postures for caring educators, which are related to receptiveness and responsiveness, and which I would frame as mindfulness qualities for management educators:

1. Cognitive and emotional availability.
2. Empathy.
3. Attentiveness.
4. Safeguarding.
5. Discretion.
6. Holding space.
7. Nourishing positive healthy sentiments (trust, acceptance, confidence).
8. Reflection/Self-reflection.

By modelling these relational postures or mindfulness qualities, the educator shifts students' thinking and understanding of leadership too. The educator demonstrates the becoming and being of a leader through the lens of care. Humanised leadership is the term recently associated with ethics of care in leadership (Klitmøller and Ernst, 2022). Perhaps, introducing and teaching mindfulness in business school learning and teaching could be framed as a pedagogy of humanised leadership. The concept of humanised leadership is considered as value-based leadership with multiple intelligences at its core, including emotional, cultural, and spiritual intelligence (Azman et al. 2023). The authors argue that spiritual and moral intelligence enables individuals to lead with integrity, honesty, and responsibility instead of greed and the desire to fulfil a personal agenda. Remember, in Chapter 1, we explored hindrances to being mindful, which include *greed* and *desire*.

The three pedagogies resonate with the philosophy and argumentation, emphasising the need to introduce and teach mindfulness in business school curriculum. All three pedagogies underpin the forthcoming chapters in the *How* section.

Chapter 3 in a nutshell...

The purpose of marrying mindfulness and business education is to support the personal and professional development of future leaders towards being more self-aware, resilient individuals. Openness to new perspectives, new ways of knowing, thinking, and being plays a crucial part in this endeavour and can lead to increased ethical decision making. Futhermore, mindfulness enhances emotional intelligence, which is paramount to becoming more self-aware. However, all of this needs to be taught in an experiential and practical manner so that students can embody it and feel it and not just learn about mindfulness in business contexts conceptually. Lived experiences are the key to transformation. Thus, the application of experiential learning with contemplative pedagogies, pedagogy of care, and humanised leadership is an essential cornerstone for mindfulness and business education to be effective. This requires training for those who are committed to being part of developing future leaders, which should be anyone facilitating learning and teaching in business schools. Educators need to be equipped with the relevant skills, competencies, and knowledge to drive a new way of doing business. I would like to close Chapter 3 with the following quotation from the *Bhagavad Gita*, (Easwaran, 2007, p.127): '*The immature think that knowledge and action are different, but the wise see them as the same. The goal of knowledge and the goal of service are the same, those who fail to see this are blind*' (*Bhagavad Gita*, 5 Rounce & Rejoice).

References

Asthana, A. N. (2021). Effectiveness of mindfulness in business education: Evidence from a controlled experiment. *International Journal of Management Education*, 19(2), Article 100492.

Asthana, A. N. (2023). Prosocial behavior of MBA students: The role of yoga and mindfulness. *Journal of Education for Business*, 98(7), 378–386. https://doi.org/10.1080/08832323.2023.2208811.

Azman, A. W., Ghani, Z. A., & Mustafah, Y. M., & Office of Knowledge for Change and Advancement. (2023). *Humanising Leadership. Transforming the Education Landscape*. International Islamic University Malaysia. https://www.iium.edu.my/media/86044/Humanising%20Leadership%20with%20e-ISBN.pdf.

Baer, R. A., Smith, G. T., Hopkins, J., Krietemeyer, J., & Toney, L. (2006). Using self-report assessment methods to explore facets of mindfulness. *Assessment*, 13(1), 27–45.

Bloom, S. G. (2022). *A second look at the blue-eyes, brown-eyes experiment that taught third-graders about racism*. The Conversation. https://theconversation.com/a-second-look-at-the-blue-eyes-brown-eyes-experiment-that-taught-third-graders-about-racism-177430.
Borker, D. R. (2013). Mindfulness practices for accounting and business education: A new perspective. *American Journal of Business Education*, 6(1), 41–56.
Bowden, J. L.-H., Tickle, L., & Naumann, K. (2021). The four pillars of tertiary student engagement and success: a holistic measurement approach. *Studies in Higher Education*, 46(6), 1207–1224.
Brown, K. W. & Ryan, R. M. (2003). The benefits of being present: Mindfulness and its role in psychological well-being. *Journal of Personality and Social Psychology*, 84(4), 822–848.
Burton, N., Culham, T., & Vu, M. C. (2021). Spiritual practice and management education pedagogy: Exploring the philosophical foundations of three spiritual traditions. *Journal of Management Education*, 45(2), 206–242. https://doi.org/10.1177/1052562920945739.
Chiang, E. P., & Sumell, A. J. (2019). Are your students absent, not absent, or present? Mindfulness and student performance. *The Journal of Economic Education*, 50(1), 1–16.
Culham, T. E. (2013). *Ethics Education of Business Leaders: Emotional Intelligence, Virtues, and Contemplative Learning*. Information Age Publishing. https://books.google.co.uk/books?id=kNN6ngEACAAJ.
Dean, K. L., Wright, S., & Forray, J. M. (2020). Experiential learning and the moral duty of business schools. *Academy of Management Learning & Education*, 19(4), 569–583.
Doty, J. R. (2016). *Into the Magic Shop: A Neurosurgeon's Quest to Discover the Mysteries of the Brain and the Secrets of the Heart*. Penguin.
Easwaran, E. (2007). *The Bhagavad Gita*. Nilgiri Press.
Ergas, O., & Hadar, L. L. (2019). Mindfulness in and as education: A map of a developing academic discourse from 2002 to 2017. *Review of Education*, 7(3), 757–797.
Eurich, T. (2017). *Insight: Why we're not as self-aware as we think, and how seeing ourselves clearly helps us succeed at work and in life*. Currency.
Gazzaley, A., & Rosen, L. D. (2016). *The distracted mind: Ancient brains in a high-tech world*. MIT Press.
Gelles, D. (2015). *Mindful work: How meditation is changing business from the inside out*. Houghton Mifflin Harcourt.
Hadar, L. L., & Ergas, O. (2022). Mindfulness for in-service and preservice teachers: an empirical map of the discourse from 2000 to 2020. *European Journal of Teacher Education*, 1–20. https://doi.org/10.1080/02619768.2022.2153669.
Harajli, D. A., & Norré, B. F. (2023). Should mindfulness practices be mandatory in business education? In P. Kumar, T. E. Culham, R. J. Major, & R. Peregoy (Eds.) *Honing self-awareness of faculty and future business leaders: Emotions connected with teaching and learning* (pp. 39–57). Emerald Publishing Limited.
Hibbert, P., & Cunliffe, A. (2015). Responsible management: Engaging moral reflexive practice through threshold concepts. *Journal of business ethics*, 127, 177–188.
Hoomans, J. (2015). *35000 Decisions: The great choices of strategic leaders*. Leading Edge. https://go.roberts.edu/leadingedge/the-great-choices-of-strategic-leaders.
Kahneman, D. (2011). *Thinking, fast and slow*. Penguin Books.
Kay, A. A., & Young, T. (2022). Distanced from others, connected to self: Online mindfulness training fosters psychological well-being by cultivating authenticity. *Academy of Management Learning & Education*, 21(2), 261–281.

Klitmøller, A., & Ernst, J. (2022, December 11–13). *An ethics of care in leadership: Humanised leadership in organizations immersed in neoliberal regimes?* [Conference presentation]. 20th International Studying Leadership Conference, Brighton, UK.

Kuechler, W., & Stedham, Y. (2018). Management education and transformational learning: The integration of mindfulness in an MBA course. *Journal of Management Education*, 42(1), 8–33.

Lampe, M., & Engleman-Lampe, C. (2012). Mindfulness-based business ethics education. *Academy of Educational Leadership Journal*, 16(3), 99–111. https://www.proquest.com/scholarly-journals/mindfulness-based-business-ethics-education/docview/1037691837/se-2?accountid=17256 https://libkey.io/libraries/2269/openurl?genre=article&au=Lampe%2C+Marc%3BEngleman-Lampe%2C+Crystal&aulast=Lampe&issn=10956328&isbn=&title=MINDFULNESS-BASED+BUSINESS+ETHICS+EDUCATION&jtitle=Academy+of+Educational+Leadership+Journal&pubname=Academy+of+Educational+Leadership+Journal&btitle=&atitle=MINDFULNESS-BASED+BUSINESS+ETHICS+EDUCATION&volume=16&issue=3&spage=99&date=2012&doi=&sid=ProQuest.

Marques, J. (2007). *The awakened leader: One simple leadership style that works every time, everywhere.* Personhood Press.

McGhee, P., & Grant, P. (2015). The influence of managers' spiritual mindfulness on ethical behaviour in organisations. *Journal of Spirituality, Leadership and Management*, 8(1), 12–33.

Mortari, L. (2016). For a pedagogy of care. *Philosophy Study*, 6(8). 455–463.

Northouse, P. G. (2021). *Leadership: Theory and practice.* Sage Publications.

Reynolds, M., & Vince, R. (2007). *Handbook of experiential learning and management education.* OUP Oxford.

Rivers, C. (2021). Active digital design 2.0. University of Surrey, Centre for Management Education. https://blogs.surrey.ac.uk/centre-management-education/2021/01/06/active-digital-design-2-0-and-add-working-group/.

Roberts, C. (2021). Developing mindful leaders: An experiential learning project. *Business Education Innovation Journal*, 13(1). 134–145.

Robertson, L. (2018). Toward an epistemology of active learning in higher education and its promise. In A. Misseyanni, M. D. Lytras, P. Papadopoulou, & C. Marouli (Eds.), *Active learning strategies in higher education: Teaching for leadership, innovation, and creativity* (pp. 17–44). Emerald Publishing Limited.

Sadler-Smith, E., & Shefy, E. (2007). Developing intuitive awareness in management education. *Academy of Management Learning & Education*, 6(2), 186–205.

Schultz, P. P., & Ryan, R. M. (2015). The 'why,' 'what,' and 'how' of healthy self-regulation: Mindfulness and well-being from a self-determination theory perspective. In B. D. Ostafin, M. D. Robinson, & B. P. Meier (Eds.), *Handbook of mindfulness and self-regulation*, (pp. 81–94). Springer.

Sezer, O., Gino, F., & Bazerman, M. H. (2015). Ethical blind spots: Explaining unintentional unethical behavior. *Current Opinion in Psychology*, 6, 77–81.

Taylor, V. F., & Bishop, K. (2019). Bringing mindfulness practice to leadership and business education. *Journal of Leadership, Accountability and Ethics*, 16(5). https://articlearchives.co/index.php/JLAE/article/view/3844.

Town, S., Reina, C. S., Brummans, B. H., & Pirson, M. (2024). Humanistic organizing: The transformative force of mindful organizational communication. *Academy of Management Review.* https://doi.org/10.5465/amr.2021.0433.

University of Northern Iowa. (2020, June 19). *Jane Elliott's Brown Eye/Blue Eye Test* [Video]. YouTube. https://www.youtube.com/watch?v=yTYL7NK8j5Y.

Vu, M. C., & Burton, N. (2020). Mindful reflexivity: Unpacking the process of transformative learning in mindfulness and discernment. *Management Learning*, 51(2), 207–226. https://doi.org/10.1177/1350507619888751.

Zajonc, A. (2013). Contemplative pedagogy: A quiet revolution in higher education. *New Directions for Teaching and Learning*, 2013(134), 83–94. https://doi.org/10.1002/tl.20057.

4

CONTEXTUALISING MINDFULNESS AND CONTEMPORARY BUSINESS TOPICS

While mindfulness can be used as a mechanism to engage students, support students on their learning journey, and help students understand themselves, more recently mindfulness has also featured in various strategic business areas to improve policymaking, regulations, and standards. It is particularly popular in the context of meeting sustainability, climate change, employee wellbeing, social responsibility, and diversity, equity, and inclusion (DEI) goals and even in recent debates around the use of artificial intelligence (AI). This chapter briefly outlines what mindfulness can add to these key areas concerning businesses and policymaking and what students might gain if mindfulness enters a dialogic intercourse with such topics.

4.1 Employee wellbeing and mindfulness

Improving employee wellbeing through mindfulness initiatives is a widely researched and well-understood area. This section only gives a very short overview of the use of mindfulness in the context of improving employee wellbeing and its benefit to business education. From Google to Goldman Sachs and the US Army, mindfulness has been recognised as enhancing employee wellbeing (Gelles, 2015). The benefits experienced by individuals and organisations have led organisations to embed mindfulness as part of their employee benefit and wellbeing policy (Slutsky et al., 2019; Wolever et al., 2018; Zivnuska et al., 2016). Due to increased staff turnover, burnout and work stress-related sick leave or long-term absenteeism, employee wellbeing has increasingly become a topic of interest for managers and leaders in human resources because absenteeism negatively impacts the performance and productivity of businesses. Burnout and stress are the two most stated reasons for absenteeism caused by work–life conflicts and too much workload (Wolever et al., 2018). Research has shown that mindfulness training offered over a period of four to six weeks led to increased physical, emotional, mental, and spiritual benefits for employees, which in turn had a positive impact on individual job performance and satisfaction and therefore organisation performance and productivity. Physical benefits of mindfulness initiatives such as meditation and mindfulness-based stress reduction alters employees brain waves (Fox & Cahn, 2021) and improves heart rate variability (Brinkmann et al., 2020) leading to employees feeling calmer and less stressed. Regular mindfulness training and, in particular, mindful organising in the workplace has been found to shift how work is experienced by employees and change attitudes towards work (Gajda & Zbierowski, 2022; Malinowski & Lim, 2015). At an emotional level, mindfulness practices led to enhanced emotional intelligence among managers and increased compassion for self and others (Adhia et al., 2010) while spirituality has also been found to increase among employees who practise mindfulness regularly (Petchsawang & McLean, 2017).

Understanding the benefits of mindfulness initiatives on employee wellbeing can help students develop higher internal and external self-awareness and an appreciation for mindfulness practices, which they would not have been able to do otherwise. Furthermore, sharing insights and knowledge on the positive impact of mindfulness initiatives and practices and engaging students in dialogue and in self-practice, enabling students to experience the benefits themselves, provides students with an invaluable toolbox to address their own work-life conflicts, proactively identify potential stressors for burnout before they arise, and notice signs of disease at work and patterns of reduced performance and productivity among colleagues. It should become a standard topic for any business management course and certainly for those concerned with people management and employee relations. In particular, programmes and courses that focus on learning and development, human resource management, organisational psychology, and occupational health must include mindfulness as a subject of learning and teaching even if it is only theoretically discussed.

4.2 Sustainability and mindfulness

Similar to employee wellbeing, businesses are increasingly concerned with sustainability and are often under pressure to find innovative solutions to address social, economic, and environmental sustainability issues. Most recently the role of mindfulness in the climate change debate and specifically climate adaption has received attention. It is believed that technology and governments alone will not be able to address the climate crisis, but a change in world views, from materialist to ecological values, might (Ericson et al., 2014; Wamsler & Brink, 2018). It is no secret that this perception has reached leaders attending the World Economic Forum, where mindfulness sessions offered are usually fully booked. Jon Kabatt-Zinn's famous statement, cited by Purser (2029) and already referred to in Chapter 3, emphasises the desperate situation we find ourselves in: 'mindfulness might be the only way for humankind and the planet to survive the next hundred years'. Only if we change our world views, our beliefs through inner work can we address sustainability challenges properly. Research conducted by Wamsler and Brink (2018) found that participants who scored highly on mindfulness questions were more motivated to engage in climate adaption activities. Adaption activities include pro-environmental and compassionate attitudes and practices, engaging in conversations with neighbours, friends, and family about sustainable lifestyle choices, intentions and actions, which might include vegetarianism and sustainable consumption of goods and services to name a few. Mindfulness is integral in facilitating this shift of private adaption (Wamsler, 2018). This shift and inner transition needs to spread from private to public adaptation, education, and governance (Ericson et al., 2014; Frank et al., 2020; Wamsler, 2018). Advocates in the field are under no illusion about the fact that this shift presents a variety of obstacles before mindfulness becomes a double dividend policy (Ericson et al., 2014). Western society is inundated with advertising and communications about norms, standards for what wellbeing, happiness, and sustainable living mean. Such advertising and communications are incessantly luring people into the belief that material consumption is more powerful than investing in mindfulness practice to save the planet. The conundrum is that material consumption is a form of escaping negativity, feeling bad or unhappy. Whereas mindfulness, at first, does not offer escape from discomfort. In fact, it suggests *sitting* with inner discomfort, becoming aware of discomfort in the present moment. Over time though, this connection to self enables the development of new values and beliefs and the growth of compassion towards self and others. It is in that process that mindfulness practice opens new perspectives towards sustainability and allows the development of mindsets for sustainability (Wamsler and Brink, 2018).

Providing a space for management students to explore such new pathways for the development of sustainability mindsets requires commitment and for the business educator to also have an openness to such world views or a desire to engage students in such conversations. In the educational realm this desire is supported by the United Nations Principles of Responsible Management Education (UN PRME; www.unprme.org) and the drive to share and teach in line with sustainable development goals (SDGs). At the heart of UN PRME and SDGs is the understanding that all people have the right to live in dignity and to meet their needs in a way that does not jeopardise the same for future generations. Business schools have a responsibility to educate and develop people who are committed to creating and sustaining inclusive organisational and societal ecosystems. The United Nations' 17 SDGs (United Nations, Department of Economic and Social Affairs, n.d.) provide the basis for this promise and include gender equality and peace, justice and strong institutions.

4.3 DEI and mindfulness

In addition to the United Nations' commitment to responsible management education and sustainable development, DEI has gained attention in board meetings, entered learning and development training, and has become a strategic goal for many companies, so much so that there is an influx of DEI directors and managers globally. Diversity in the workplace refers to the plethora of individual human differences present in an organisation such as race, gender, ethnicity, or age. Equity emphasises the need for equal opportunities and equal access to services for all employees regardless of such differences. Inclusion in the workplace focuses on creating a culture of belonging for all employees through mechanisms and fora that enable all employees to be heard and respected.

Several events might have contributed to the rise of DEI in organisations and education, including the death of George Floyd, the Black Lives Matter movement, and public conversations about the gender pay gap and the Covid pandemic. The latter, in particular, has led to a collective empathy and compassion towards self and others. At a time when the world appeared upside down, mindfulness became an anchor for many to navigate the turmoil because mindfulness is equitable and inclusive to each and every one of us regardless of race, gender, ethnicity, income, or age (Bautista et al., 2022). However, mindfulness is not always equally accessible. Similarly, we often believe that mindfulness workshops are inclusive too, but this depends on the relationship one has with mindfulness. As business educators, we have the opportunity to give students from diverse backgrounds access to mindfulness in an equitable and inclusive way. The concept of DEI is a great vehicle to engage students in the classroom, not just theoretically but practically in the debate and experience. DEI training has to start in the classroom (Sánchez-Flores, 2017). Through self-reflection and self-awareness students gain awareness of different sources of privilege and disadvantage. The exploration of their own dimensions of identity helps students understand their own position in society in comparison to others (e.g. privilege and disadvantage) and to develop an appreciation for their own situation while becoming compassionate towards self and others. The latter is particularly important in order to address DEI experientially rather than conceptually. Mindfulness and meditation are key elements of DEI training with students to cultivate compassion (Sánchez-Flores, 2017). Mindfulness practices have increased the self-awareness of participants and enabled participants to also become aware of their involvement in creating inequitable situations or utilising their privilege in a way that disadvantages others. Thus, mindfulness plays a pivotal role in creating inclusive workplaces, and it starts with educating future leaders adequately by equipping future leaders with the right skills (Goldman Schuyler et al., 2021). We can only respond to our environment in a way that we have learned to respond because our behaviour and knowledge is socially constructed. Compassion and love are not concepts or skills explicitly taught in school or higher education, so we cannot expect future leaders to act in a responsible and compassionate way if they are not aware of the impact of their own actions and if they do not have a toolbox to change their behaviour or influence others. Thus, it is not surprising that executives who have never learned to act compassionately towards themselves and others do not know how to adopt a mindful way of being towards human resources or the planet. Integrating mindfulness into the curriculum requires a mindset shift from traditional management education to humanistic management education, from mindfulness as a technique to reduce stress with the purpose of increasing employee performance to mindfulness practices that are rooted in wisdom tradition (generative mindfulness), and from DEI as a tick-box exercise to a willingness to create inclusive workplaces (Goldman Schuyler et al., 2021). Generative mindfulness is understood 'as the process of waking up to one's interconnectedness with all other living beings within the context of culture and society' (Goldman Schuyler et al., 2021, p .455) and perhaps AI can support this endeavour in the future.

4.4 Artificial intelligence and mindfulness

In 2021, I wrote a book chapter with a colleague about how AI might be used in business education to support student learning and assist business educators (Rivers & Holland, 2022). At the time our understanding about what AI is capable of and the importance of it in business education and specifically in developing future leaders was limited. We would not have been able to anticipate how AI disrupted our learning and teaching space. Since then, many debates have taken place across business schools, at conferences and dedicated AI webinars, to untangle the rise and impact of AI in business education and beyond. Professional bodies have also tried to make sense of and provide guidance about the use of AI in learning and teaching contexts and how such technologies would transform business education (AACSB Business Education Intelligence, 2023; AACSB Thought Leadership, 2023). Most concerns surrounded the use of AI for assessments, marking (Gardner et al., 2021), and publishing (Medvedev & Krägeloh, 2023) and how to retain academic integrity (Cotton et al., 2023). Further along the way, business educators expressed the need to educate students about the responsible use of AI throughout their studies (Rosenboom, 2023) and invite employers to expand students' sense of responsible AI use beyond their academic endeavours (Hogg, 2019; Pandya et al., 2022). The discussions led to a cultural divide among educators, those who embrace and those who reject AI for learning and teaching purposes. Students also voiced their views about the use of AI and adopted similar embrace/reject perspectives (Smolansky et al., 2023). Regardless of the debates and opinions, we all know that AI is here to stay.

It is fair to say that AI disrupted business education in an unexpected way, causing fear, worry, doubt, and a desire for AI to disappear in the business school community. In Chapter 1, the fourth foundation of mindfulness, *mindfulness of Dharma* referred to fear, worry, doubt, and desire as hindrances that cause human suffering. The way to address suffering rooted in fear, worry, doubt, and desire is to investigate and identify the root of suffering. While such investigation might be helpful to truly understand the reasons for our own fears, such as AI replacing our profession and ultimately becoming smarter than us, it also seems important to include in the investigation how AI relates to other intelligences, human intelligences, so we can learn to co-exist in a mindful relationship that is mutually beneficially. AI is part of our reality now and some might even say that AI is equivalent to aspects of human intelligence having been adopted by machines (Huang & Rust, 2018). This statement is particularly interesting in the context of intelligence being understood as 'biopsychological potential that all individuals possess by virtue of being human' (Davis et al., 2011, p. 492).

Earlier in the book, I reframed mindfulness as an innate human intelligence and referred to it as awareness intelligence, which aligns with the above reference to intelligence as a biopsychological potential. Awareness intelligence combines somatic and emotional intelligence and self-awareness in the pursuit of accessing present moment experiences. Focusing our attention on the present moment is an ability we are born with. Therefore, we do have the capacity to develop it into a skill that can be cultivated through regular practice and that can serve us in our quest to develop inclusive future leaders. In fact, mastering awareness intelligence is a must-have skill for future leaders.

While our present moment experience cannot be replicated or accessed by AI systems, we might use AI to support the process of becoming self-aware in the present moment. Various industries have turned the capabilities of AI into profitable opportunities (Wang & Uysal, 2023) and sometimes it is more about reminding ourselves to be mindful. This reminding ourselves to be mindful can be hard, much harder than the intention to be mindful (Goldstein, 2013). Although the awareness intelligence that we experience during meditation is untouchable by AI and therefore unique to us humans, we might be able to harness AI in a way to support us on our journey to becoming more mindful. For instance, we might be able to use AI in a way to make us aware of our physical sensations through providing instant information about body temperature, heart rate, oxygen levels, brain activity when we are experiencing stress and use AI to support us in human-to-human interaction. While AI would not be able, and neither would we, to know what a person is really thinking or feeling and anticipate reactions, AI can support us in managing our emotions and therefore reactions through prompts deduced from bodily measurements. We have the ability, through awareness intelligence, to open a channel for compassion and empathy that connects us with others on a different level in the present moment, but we need help to learn to use it in a similar way to how we would train any other human intelligence.

In 1983, Professor Howard Gardner introduced the theory of multiple intelligences, which he developed from decades of research. Seven intelligences were identified to meet the criteria of intelligence (Davis et al., 2011), which are inherent in every human and develop differently over time: visual intelligence, linguistic intelligence, mathematical intelligence, musical intelligence, bodily-kinaesthetic intelligence, interpersonal intelligence, intrapersonal intelligence, and naturalistic intelligence (Gardner, 1993). Some of these intelligences are already successfully performed by AI systems, which has led to despair and the need for regulation (e.g. writing music, creating paintings, speeches, screenplays). Yet, all of these aspects are externally oriented and based on information available to an AI system from which it can draw conclusions and interact with humans. So, the question is how can we use AI in a responsible and ethical way to support our own evolution? I believe that AI has a lot to offer in conjunction with mindfulness.

AI does not have to be a threat if we choose to use it wisely. Even though AI can learn, it is unable to become aware of its own existence in such a way that it would question its purpose or become reflective about its actions, thoughts, and feelings because these do not exist and there is no need for AI to develop and have an awareness intelligence. It seems that the word intelligence has grown into something we believe exists, like a *thing*, because we believe we can measure and label intelligences. Intelligences are *only* scientific constructs, created to make sense of something intangible and unexplainable otherwise. Gardner (1993) emphasises that the list of intelligences is infinite. In fact, we have already moved from AI to artificial super intelligence (ASI). Regardless of how many super intelligences have one day been created, only if we develop the ability to cultivate our awareness intelligence rightfully will we be able to lead responsibly in the future.

The question that we need to ask ourselves and our students is what relationship would you like to have with AI? My colleague Anna Holland and I (Rivers & Holland, 2024) explored this question in a recent podcast recorded for the Management Education and Development, Academy of Management podcast series *mEDucation unlocked* in March 2024. We discuss this aspect of identifying our relationship with AI and how we need to bring this discourse into the classroom. We propose an intentional, conscious, and mindful approach towards reframing our relationship with AI. Intentional refers to the motivation of using AI, conscious is about knowing and experiencing the mental states that arise and exist while using AI, and mindful is practising being present in the process, present in the body, present in the mind and heart. Such an approach enables future leaders to become creative and curious about their thoughts, actions and emotions while using AI to optimise business processes or make decisions, but it also encourages future leaders to evaluate their decisions based on AI more carefully and to foresee potential consequences.

Chapter 4 in a nutshell...

The contextualisation of mindfulness in contemporary business topics and themes requires careful consideration especially in terms of access and delivery, to be equitable and generative. Exploring mindfulness in the context of employee wellbeing, sustainability, and questions of diversity and even AI has been found to increase self-awareness and compassion among students towards self, others, technology use, and the environment, but again, it requires the right skills and knowledge of facilitators to cultivate a sense of responsibility in the mind of future leaders. Engaging students in dialogue and exploring the connection between mindfulness and pressing societal concepts and debates shapes their own beliefs, values, and understanding of the world of work as a network of people and technology systems. Thus, contextualising mindfulness in contemporary business topics can be a useful learning and teaching strategy to increase student self-awareness and non-intellectual reflective practice and emotional intelligence.

I would like to close Chapter 4 with two quotes. Both quotes emphasise that business education is a safe space for students to explore and reflect upon how we can let go of what does not serve us in the future and that there is no need to lead with anger and greed or fight to satisfy selfish desire. The topics touched upon in this chapter symbolise gateways to attaining business goals that serve society. The first quote is adapted from the *Bhagavad Gita* (Easwaran, 2007, p. 241,: '*There are three gates of self-destruction: lust, anger and greed. Driven by selfish desire they miss the goal of life, miss even happiness and success. Those who escape from these three gates, seek what is best and attain life's goal.*' (*Bhagavad Gita*, 16 Two Paths) and the second is a Native American proverb. '*No tree has branches so foolish as to fight amongst themselves.*' (World of Proverbs, n.d.).

References

AACSB Business Education Intelligence. (2023). Technologies with potential to transform business and business education. https://www.aacsb.edu/insights/briefings/artificial-intelligence.

AACSB Thought Leadership. (2023). Business school innovation in the age of generative AI. https://www.aacsb.edu/insights/briefings/business-school-innovation-in-the-age-of-generative-ai.

Adhia, H., Nagendra, H., & Mahadevan, B. (2010). Impact of adoption of yoga way of life on the emotional intelligence of managers. *IIMB Management Review*, 22(1–2), 32–41.

Bautista, T., Cash, T., Meyerhoefer, T., & Pipe, T. (2022). Equitable Mindfulness: The practice of mindfulness for all. *Journal of Community Psychology*, 50(7), 3141–3155.

Brinkmann, A. E., Press, S. A., Helmert, E., Hautzinger, M., Khazan, I., & Vagedes, J. (2020). Comparing effectiveness of HRV-biofeedback and mindfulness for workplace stress reduction: A randomized controlled trial. *Applied psychophysiology and biofeedback*, 45, 307–322. https://www.ncbi.nlm.nih.gov/pmc/articles/PMC7644531/pdf/10484_2020_Article_9477.pdf.

Cotton, D. R., Cotton, P. A., & Shipway, J. R. (2023). Chatting and cheating: Ensuring academic integrity in the era of ChatGPT. *Innovations in Education and Teaching International*, 61(2), 228–239.

Davis, K., Christodoulou, J., Seider, S., & Gardner, H. E. (2011). The theory of multiple intelligences. In R. J. Sternberg, & S. B. Kaufman (Eds.), *Cambridge Handbook of Intelligence* (pp. 485–503). Cambridge University Press.

Easwaran, E. (2007). *The Bhagavad Gita*. Nilgiri Press.

Ericson, T., Kjønstad, B. G., & Barstad, A. (2014). Mindfulness and sustainability. *Ecological Economics*, 104, 73–79.

Fox, K. C., & Cahn, B. R. (2021). Meditation and the brain in health and disease. In M. Farias, D. Brazier, M. Lalljee, (Eds.), *The Oxford Handbook of Meditation* (pp. 429–461). Oxford University Press.

Frank, P., Fischer, D., & Wamsler, C. (2020). Mindfulness, education, and the sustainable development goals. In W. Leal Filho, A. M. Azul, L. Brandly, P.Gökçin Özuyar, & T. Wall (Eds.), *Quality Education* (pp. 545–555). Springer.

Gajda, D., & Zbierowski, P. (2022). Exploring the consequences of mindfulness at work: the impact of mindful organizing on employee attitudes and behavior toward work and organization. *Personnel Review*, 52(9). 2342–2362.

Gardner, H. (1993). *Multiple intelligences. The theory in practice*. Basic books.

Gardner, J., O'Leary, M., & Yuan, L. (2021). Artificial intelligence in educational assessment:'Breakthrough? Or buncombe and ballyhoo?'. *Journal of Computer Assisted Learning*, 37(5), 1207–1216.

Gelles, D. (2015). *Mindful work: How meditation is changing business from the inside out*. Houghton Mifflin Harcourt.

Goldman Schuyler, K., Watson, L. W., & King, E. (2021). How generative mindfulness can contribute to inclusive workplaces. *Humanistic Management Journal*, 6(3), 451–478.

Goldstein, J. (2013). *Mindfulness: A practical guide to awakening*. Sounds True.

Hogg, P. (2019). Artificial intelligence: HR friend or foe? *Strategic HR Review*, 18(2), 47–51.

Huang, M.-H., & Rust, R. T. (2018). Artificial intelligence in service. *Journal of service research*, 21(2), 155–172.

Malinowski, P., & Lim, H. J. (2015). Mindfulness at work: Positive affect, hope, and optimism mediate the relationship between dispositional mindfulness, work engagement, and well-being. *Mindfulness*, 6, 1250–1262.

Medvedev, O., & Krägeloh, C. (2023). Harnessing artificial intelligence for mindfulness research and dissemination: Guidelines for authors. *Mindfulness*, 14, 1019–1020.

Pandya, B., Patterson, L., & Ruhi, U. (2022). The readiness of workforce for the world of work in 2030: perceptions of university students. *International Journal of Business Performance Management*, 23(1–2), 54–75.

Petchsawang, P., & McLean, G. N. (2017). Workplace spirituality, mindfulness meditation, and work engagement. *Journal of Management, Spirituality & Religion*, 14(3), 216–244.

Purser, R. (2019). The mindfulness conspiracy. *The Guardian*. https://www.theguardian.com/lifeandstyle/2019/jun/14/the-mindfulness-conspiracy-capitalist-spirituality.

Rivers, C., & Holland, A. (2022). Management education and artificial intelligence: Toward personalized learning. In M. R. Fellenz, S. Hoidn, & M. Brady (Eds.), *The future of management education* (pp. 184–204). Routledge.

Rivers, C., Holland, A.; Nolan E. (Hosts). (2024–present). Embracing AI in education: navigating intentions, integrity, and human consciousness [Audio podcast]. mEDucation unlocked: The podcast series. M. E. a. D. D. Academy of

Management. https://open.spotify.com/episode/2lisPhnO5yKPW0HLIn3SHI?go= 1&sp_cid=20091329eefba603ed0c65792fd6b538&intent=addToLibrary&utm_ source=embed_player_v&utm_medium=desktop&nd=1&dlsi=c76c45e17a36417e.

Rosenboom, A. (2023). Marketing and artificial intelligence: Responsible management (and marketing) education at the nexus of today and tomorrow. In C. Hauser, & W. Amann (Eds.), *The future of responsible management education: University leadership and the digital transformation challenge* (pp. 115–137). Springer.

Sánchez-Flores, M. J. (2017). Mindfulness and complex identities in equity training: a pilot study. *European review of applied sociology*, 10(14), 20–33.

Slutsky, J., Chin, B., Raye, J., & Creswell, J. D. (2019). Mindfulness training improves employee well-being: A randomized controlled trial. *J Occup Health Psychol*, 24(1), 139–149. https://doi.org/10.1037/ocp0000132.

Smolansky, A., Cram, A., Raduescu, C., Zeivots, S., Huber, E., & Kizilcec, R. F. (2023). Educator and student perspectives on the impact of generative AI on assessments in higher education. In *Proceedings of the Tenth ACM Conference on Learning@ Scale* (pp. 378–382). Association for Computing Machinery. https://doi.org/10.1145/3573051.3596191.

United Nations, Department for Economic and Social Affairs. Sustainable Development. (n.d.). *The 17 Goals.* RetrievedAugust 2, 2024, fromhttps://sdgs.un.org/goals.

Wamsler, C. (2018). Mind the gap: The role of mindfulness in adapting to increasing risk and climate change. *Sustainability Science*, 13, 1121–1135.

Wamsler, C., & Brink, E. (2018). Mindsets for sustainability: Exploring the link between mindfulness and sustainable climate adaptation. *Ecological Economics*, 151, 55–61.

Wang, Y.-C., & Uysal, M. (2023). Artificial intelligence-assisted mindfulness in tourism, hospitality, and events. *International Journal of Contemporary Hospitality Management*, 36(4), 1262–1278.

Wolever, R. Q., Schwartz, E. R., & Schoenberg, P. L. (2018). Mindfulness in corporate America: Is the Trojan horse ethical? *The Journal of Alternative and Complementary Medicine*, 24(5), 403–406.

World of Proverbs. (n.d.). *Native American Proverb 19633.* Retrieved August 2, 2024, from https://www.worldofproverbs.com/2012/12/no-tree-has-branches-so-foolish-as-to.html.

Zivnuska, S., Kacmar, K. M., Ferguson, M., & Carlson, D. S. (2016). Mindfulness at work: Resource accumulation, well-being, and attitudes. *Career Development International*, 21(2), 106–124.

PART III
How to bring mindfulness and business education to life

5
MINDFULNESS AS EXTRACURRICULAR ACTIVITY

5.1 Engagement and commitment challenge

When I started to research how business schools engage with mindfulness or offer mindfulness sessions to their students, it became clear that mindfulness is not necessarily a topic business schools are too familiar with. Instead, as pointed out in previous chapters, there are individual academics who are familiar with mindfulness practice and therefore informally introduce concepts and techniques to their students outside the classroom as an extracurricular activity. In some instances, these informal services turned into more formalised sessions accessible to a whole cohort. Extracurricular activities have received little attention in the literature, and the definition of *extracurricular* is believed to be self-explanatory. In this chapter, I define extracurricular as an event or session offered outside the usual timetable of a learner and not linked to the curriculum. Participation is purely intrinsically motivated, and extracurricular activities serve personal development rather than academic development. However, they are not mutually exclusive. Attendance is neither monitored nor compulsory, and there are no assignments or certificates for students upon completion. In some schools, students can collect badges for attending extracurricular activities, which might enable students to receive an award at the end of their degree which is linked to employability attributes and personal development. However, in my experience mindfulness rarely features in such schemes. We will address opportunities for embedding mindfulness strategically in educational policy in Chapter 9.

The optional and seemingly unrelated nature of extracurricular activities in comparison to co-curricular activities (Bartkus et al., 2012) highlights challenges such as engagement, commitment and attendance. In my conversations with business school leaders, frustration has been voiced about the lack of engagement from students in extracurricular activities in comparison to the effort and investment involved in designing and facilitating events. A study conducted in Australia on engagement levels of business students in extracurricular activities confirmed the devastating experience academics and practitioners can have Hitchcock et al. (2024). The authors shared that 300 out of 1000 students attended the first event, which was related to developing employability skills. The programme was designed in collaboration with industry professionals and academics and offered as a kick-start initiative for commencing students. However, the excitement of the initial turnout dwindled shortly after, as attendance and engagement dropped significantly throughout the semester. At the end of the semester, at the final session, only 17 students remained. The scenario resonates with my own experience of offering extracurricular activities over the length of a semester. During lockdown, I offered a 12-week online yoga and meditation programme centred around different themes that would speak to the students' study related needs, such as assessments and group work. Themes included topics such as focused, calm, connected, and creative. My intention was to use yoga and meditation as tools to support students in developing mindful relationships with themselves and others. The sessions took place on a Wednesday afternoon, which is the only afternoon during the week without teaching when, instead, students are encouraged to engage in student union activities, clubs, or sporting events. I crafted each topic and session with the university marketing team and sent out the invites via social media and email. Two-hundred and twenty-nine students signed up to join the online sessions. I asked three questions: What is your experience with yoga and meditation? What are your reasons and expectations for signing up? Do you have any injuries I need to know about? A third of the students indicated that they have a regular practice, and their main focus was to be part of a community while being confined to their rooms. Approximately another third of the students had no experience and were intrigued by the marketing material but shared that it might help them to study, stay more focused, and concentrate on what matters. The third group of students were struggling with mental and physical challenges from chronic back pain to anxiety and panic attacks. All necessary precautions were taken to ensure that students were safe and supported throughout the sessions. The Centre for Wellbeing was on standby, and I had a list of all personal tutors too. At the first session, 165 students joined via Zoom. Cameras were on and off. Throughout the class the number declined slightly, and at the end, students shared their experiences in the chat. The week after, 98 students joined the class and the week after that, 67. By the end of the 12 weeks, 11 students remained. The question is, what happened? Why does engagement reduce so dramatically? Does it mean that extracurricular activities are not worthwhile?

Despite the frustration and challenges outlined above, sufficient evidence exists that confirms the benefits of extracurricular activities for students during and after their studies. In fact, studies revealed that CEOs were often more involved in extracurricular activities during their time as business students, and some even correlated their success and effectiveness as leaders with such engagements (Boone et al., 1988). Extracurricular activities have also been found to generate a positive attitude among students towards creating businesses and being entrepreneurial. However, attendance does not necessarily translate into action (Arranz et al., 2017). Another study conducted in a business school in Finland demonstrated the impact of student-led extracurricular activities on enhancing leadership skills and particularly strengthening female cultural capital and the aspirations of female business students to attain male-dominated roles in business (Isopahkala-Bouret et al., 2023).

It is safe to say that extracurricular activities have their place, but it is paramount to understand what drives students' engagement. The studies on extracurricular activities that reported good levels of engagement and positive outcomes seem to have one aspect in common, collaboration with students in the design and promotion of such activities (e.g. student-led). Based on my own experience, there are two more aspects to consider. First, because of the nature of extracurricular activities, full semester/term-length programmes tend to be perceived as too much effort by students. Therefore, extracurricular activities must be either one-off events or short-term commitments; three weeks seems to be the threshold. Secondly, students need to be clear about the value of attending – 'what is in it for me?' and timing is crucial. For instance, offering a mindfulness session before assessment submission deadline might sound like a great idea to reduce stress and anxiety, but the offer is most likely to be rejected by students because their attention is on the assessment. However, a session after a submission deadline or at mark release, to help students manage their emotions or thoughts, is likely to be well attended. In addition, incentives, rewards, or winning a prize also increase attendance. The latter is rooted in theories of operant conditioning (Skinner, 1971) and motivation (Herzberg, 2017). Below I share the experience of one such extracurricular event that I am asked to facilitate year on year. The case study includes detailed resources, such as meditation scripts and yoga poses and coaching questions to facilitate such sessions.

5.2 'Good Enough' – leading with compassion: Case study

> *I loved being able to detach from everything for two hours, especially after I received my marks. They are not bad but not what I wanted. I was angry and disappointed and ... having some space to reflect has helped to put things in perspective.*
>
> *Claire, 21–22, Final year student*

In February 2022, I was approach by the president of the wellbeing student society, Jen, who heard about my online yoga classes for students. She shared that final year students felt stressed and inadequate, and soon marks would be released to inform students about the outcome of their degrees, which has a profound impact on what students believe their future possibilities are. For many students, mark release is a time to experience increased levels of stress and anxiety, and the outcome determines their motivation and focus for the remaining academic year. Jen shared that a lot of her fellow students simply do not feel good enough or ready to enter the world of work. '*We all have imposter syndrome,*' Jen said, and she suggested provision of a space to explore that. We agreed on a two-hour mini retreat event on the topic of *I am good enough* and to schedule the retreat for the day of mark release. A small budget allowed Jen to purchase nibbles and drinks and to pay for journals and pens. In addition, she organised a prize draw for those who signed up to win a yoga mat and some other goodies. She organised the event, created marketing materials, and communicated with peers. The mini retreat was fully booked within hours and more people turned up than expected. This was a fully booked extracurricular mindfulness event led by the students.

The structure of the mini retreat includes a combination of mediation, yoga, journaling, and reflection with coaching questions as shown in Table 5.1. The aim of the retreat is to help students rewrite their story to say what *I am good enough* means to them in the context of their course, study performance, and the profession they are pursuing. The outcome of the mini retreat is to be able to access their new narrative about themselves when they need to and to have a set of tools available to rekindle their relationship to themselves when they experience '*not good enoughness*' times. The journal gives students a tangible resource to take home and come back to. For many, it is the first time they have journaled or engaged in an experience of mindfulness. I also like to give students a coloured ribbon that can be worn on the wrist as a reminder to be mindful with themselves going forwards because, as Joseph Goldstein said: '*It's not hard to be mindful; it just takes time training to remember to be mindful*' (Goldstein, 2013, p. 231). For

TABLE 5.1 Retreat structure 'Good Enough'

Retreat structure	*Duration (in minutes)*
Opening meditation	20
Journal time	5
Yoga sequence	30
Comfort break	5
Coaching questions and individual journal	30
Sharing in small groups	20
Closing meditation	10

this retreat I use a green ribbon, which represents the colour of the heart chakra, Anahata (Perrakis, 2018). It represents the epicentre for love, kindness, acceptance, and compassion, which are the aspects surrounding the theme of not feeling good enough. When we cultivate the feeling of compassion, the heart space is a neutral place to focus on as it offers space to plant a little seed of compassion.

In collaboration with students, you might find that they ask you for your guidance to structure the workshop. I used the following format, which has been perceived well and allows students enough time to explore and remain curious. Remember most business students are not familiar with meditation, yoga, or coaching tools. Therefore, simple and short sequences are more powerful in a one-off event. Make sure you build in some comfort break time. It might not be needed, but for some the experience can be overwhelming. This gives them an opportunity to either leave or take a break and speak to their peers.

5.3 'Good Enough': Resources

Start the retreat with a 20-minute meditation to allow students to settle into the space and enable them to become present and let go of the day thus far so they can start to connect with themselves around the theme. The script below sets the scene for the retreat.

Opening meditation: 20 minutes

> Welcome. Find a comfortable seat of your choice or lie down if you prefer. Feel the connection between your sit bones and the mat, or if you are lying down, feel the connection between the back of the body and the mat. As you breathe in, lengthen through the spine, gently tuck the chin into the chest. As you breathe out, relax the shoulders and hips, and soften your gaze or close your eyes if that feels good. Feel the weight of your body on the mat. Let's do this one more time, long deep breath in through the nose and exhale; let it go.
>
> Now, bring your attention to the breath; notice your belly rising as you breathe in and retracting as you exhale. Notice how it feels. We use the breath to connect with our self, to become present and aware of how we feel right here, right now. Take a moment and feel inside you. If there is a word that described how you feel, what would it be? [30 seconds to explore] With your next exhale, let it go; see the word drift away like a cloud. Return to your normal rhythm of breath, and rest here for now.
>
> Today might have been emotional for you, maybe expected, maybe not. You might have had thoughts and feelings that you are not good enough. We all have them from time to time. Often this happens when we feel inadequate because of an outcome, an expectation that we set and have not met. The expectation might even have a story attached. You might believe that having a particular grade would change the way you feel about yourself. You might believe that a particular grade would be confirmation that you are competent and knowledgeable enough. In this scenario, your concept of being good enough is contingent on an external outcome, a condition.

We all create stories, conditions, and expectations in our mind to measure and evaluate our own *enoughness*. What we believe to be good enough is rooted in how we learned about what good enough is and whether we concluded at some point to attribute *enoughness* to who we are rather than to a particular aspect or event. How can we unlearn, change our beliefs and story about being good enough, so that we can differentiate between being good enough as a person and being good enough in a particular aspect of our life and able to still accept and believe in ourselves despite it?

Being good enough is about your relationship with yourself. How you accept yourself, self-acceptance. How you believe in yourself, self-belief and how you treat yourself, self-compassion. Throughout this retreat, we will learn to cultivate self-acceptance, self-belief, and self-compassion for who you are and apply curiosity in the process of experiencing wobbles.

Remember an event or scenario where you felt good enough, big or small. How did you feel in that moment? What words would describe that feeling? Where in your body is that feeling located? Bring your full attention to the space and place your hands on the part of the body where you feel it. If there is no particular part, then focus on your heart space and place your hands on your heart space.

With your next breath in whisper to yourself or say quietly in your head: *I am good enough, I am good enough, I am good enough*. Keep repeating the phrase while feeling your hands on the part of the body where you located the feeling and breathe into the area. With every breath, imagine that this feeling disperses into the rest of your body. [Instructor note: You can be really descriptive here to and speak about limbs, head, and so on. Give students two minutes to sit with themselves like that].

Now, let the mantra go, and allow silence to be present, to become part of you. [Instructor note: Give students another two minutes to sit in silence.] When you hear the sound of the chimes, gently open your eyes and return into the space. Take your journal and write down anything that has arisen for you.

Creating space to let thoughts come and go and expressing them externally by writing them down enables students to let go and move on. Journal time can be short, about three to five minutes, which in my experience is sufficient for the start of such events. I used to invite students to share their experiences, but at this point, they are often not comfortable doing so. It takes time to let experiences settle and establish a certain level of trust that it is okay to share, and they will not be judged. In collaboration with the students, we identified three sub-themes in relation to the topic: fear of judgement, should narrative, comparing with others, and the inner critic. Because these sub-themes are prevalent, it can be more beneficial to continue with a short yoga sequence that allows students to go deeper into the body and those sub-themes.

Yoga: 30 minutes

The yoga sequence is designed to speak to the sub-themes with the purpose of cultivating self-acceptance. Balance poses are particularly suited to address the sub-themes. I often refer to balance poses as a reflection of wobbles in life and an opportunity to embrace the wobbles in life, the things that can throw us off, like not meeting our own expectations or those of society, which in turn manifest as internal and external judgment, should narrative, comparison with others, and a strong inner critic.

Sun salutations

Begin with a number of sun salutations before moving into balance poses.

> Stand at the top of your mat in mountain pose, hands to either side of the torso, palms facing forwards. Breathe in raise your arms up towards the ceiling, and as you breathe out, forward fold. Breathe in, bring your hands to your shins or thighs, flat back. Breathe out, forward fold. Step your left foot back. Step your right foot back. Lower your knees if you need to, plank pose. Breathe in. Shift your weight forwards, and breathe out. Lower to the mat. Breathe in. Cobra or upward facing dog, and breathe out, moving into downward facing dog. Take three breaths here. With your next breath in, bend the knees, and step to the front of the mat. Forward fold. Breathe in. Press through all four corners of the feet and root to rise. Back to mountain pose.

Repeat that sequence three to five times before moving into balance poses. Figure 5.2 shows all the poses in this opening sequence.

Fear of judgment – Tree pose

Students shared that they feel anxious about applying for jobs and working in a business environment. Students who have not opted for a placement year, in particular, feel less well prepared for the world of work. Jen explained that it is more than just feeling anxious; it is a fear of being judged as not knowing enough, not having the right skills, and not being able to add value in meetings and conversations. This fear is heightened when students receive a lower mark than expected in a subject they previously thought they were good at; it shatters their confidence. To work on this sub-theme, I like to introduce tree pose as shown in Figure 5.1.

I introduce three different variations of tree pose, depending on the students' level of experience with yoga. First, we shift weight into the left foot and place the sole of the right foot on the ankle. Hands can go up to the ceiling, or students can place them in front of the heart in prayer position. We usually all start here and bring our attention to the breath and notice how it feels. I continue to invite people to either stay here or join me for the next step to bring the right foot up higher and place it on the calf. Take a moment again, stop and bring attention to the breath, and ask how it feels. At this

78 Mindfulness and Business Education

Variation 1: foot on ankle

Variation 2: foot on shin

Variation 3: foot on thigh

FIGURE 5.1 Tree pose (variations)

point it is helpful to speak to the chatter in the mind about not being able to go to the next stage or finding this variation too easy and the exercise itself silly. Emphasise that we are all at different levels of experience and ability. Invite openness and curiosity towards the experience. The final variation is to move the right foot up to the inside of the left thigh. It is important not to place the foot on the knee though, so as to avoid injury. At this stage come back to the breath and experience aspect. The left foot might also be feeling heavy at this point as you are holding the balance for a while. If you want to add a challenge for your students, ask them to close their eyes. You can see who is playful and who is anxious. It often ends in laughter and falling over, so then encourage them to get back into it, and at the same time, allow them to be playful. It is at this point that students leave the judge at the door. They explore and are curious. I love the quality of tree pose to turn the judge off and turn fear into fun. At the end, shake out the legs and take it over to the other side. Ask them to feel into the pose and how it feels different on this side.

Should narrative – Warrior Three

The judge thoughts are often accompanied by the modal verb *should*. It implies an obligation towards something rooted in an expectation, which makes it like an absolute truth, that something should be a certain way and that way is the only right way. *I should be more focused. I should be knowledgeable. I should work hard to achieve my goals.* Warrior Three is one of those poses that most people believe they should perform in a certain way, maybe because they used to do when they were children, or maybe because they expect to perform in a certain way. I use Warrior Three to break expectations and, similar to tree pose, offer a three step exploration as shown in Figure 5.2.

Mindfulness as extracurricular activity   79

Variation 1: balancing on the big toe   Variation 2: leg two inches off the floor   Variation 3: leg parallel to the floor

FIGURE 5.2 Warrior Three (variations)

Begin by shifting your weight into the left foot. Leave your hands on either side of the body. Breathe in. Bend your right leg, and lift it up, two inches off the floor to start with. With your next exhale, hinge from the hips, and lean forwards. Let your upper body guide you, and your right leg will automatically lift higher. Straighten your right leg, but do not lock the knee. We want to keep softness in the knee. You might find that your leg is lifted up and parallel to the floor, or maybe it is a little bit off the floor. If you find it really challenging, place the big toe on the floor and balance there. Stay here, and ask how it feels and whether you are expecting anything?

Invite them to go further if they feel comfortable. Bring them back to the chatter in mind as you speak to how *should* can hold us back in experiencing where we are at this moment in time. Guide them to tap into how they feel and let the feeling of *I can go further* guide them rather than *I should*. You can take it a step further and invite students to raise their hands over their heads or even move their arms in circles. Bringing playfulness into the process moves the person from the chains of *should* into aligning body and mind and letting go, embracing the present moment and all the wobbles that come with it. Slowly guide them back to mountain pose and shake out the legs before taking it over to the other side.

Comparing and the inner critic – Inviting gratitude and being playful

As you are guiding students through the poses and focusing on a particular sub-theme, you will notice that students will look at each other and the reactions of others because they feel uncertain and insecure. That is normal, and so they look for confirmation through comparison. Speak to it and invite gratitude to the moment. Encourage students to be playful and explore their thoughts and emotions.

As students play with the different variations, they focus on themselves; they become present and it reveals determination and tenacity. However, it can also give them a mirror to notice their resistance. Such exploration should be fun and embraced in a non-judgmental way. After playing around with different variations, lead students into a moment of rest. Invite students to lie on their front or back, and bring their attention back to the breath. Allow silence to settle in before moving into the next part.

Coaching and journal time: 30 minutes

When I started out designing such sessions, I used to have more meditation and yoga elements on my guidance sheet, but while working with the students, I sensed the need for more time in reflection and sharing of experiences, which they appreciated, and it enabled them to go deeper into their inner world. So, leave a considerable amount of time for introspection. The questions below are a way to support this inward journey.

- What are two or three achievements you are proud of?
- How did these achievements unfold, and did you feel enough at this point?
- What were the feelings that confirmed to you that you were good enough?
- Now, what two achievements would you like to accomplish?
- What are the worries associated with these?
- What are the expectations?
- What would it feel like to feel good enough?

Give sufficient time in between questions so that students can ponder a little bit. The questions are designed to change the way they feel about themselves. Feeling good can turn into a reward feeling, which is more powerful. After the final question, open the floor for sharing experiences, and guide them back to the feeling tone of *good enough*. I sometimes ask them to describe the feeling of *good enough* in great detail, and I use a flip chart to write down their comments. Students can find such exercises helpful because they notice they are not alone, so it positively reinforces their experience.

Before closing the workshop move into statement formulation. Ask students to complete the following sentences to help them let go of the past and move into the present moment while making an agreement, setting an actionable outcome.

- I used to believe ….
- I am …. I am good enough.
- From now on …

Worries and expectations trap us in the past and future. Thoughts of worry are learned habits (Brewer & Roy, 2021; Brewer et al., 2020) and affirmations can rewire our thoughts. If we feel anxious for instance, we might have learned that worrying thoughts reduce anxiety; it is a positive reward.

Therefore, our habit is to worry when we feel anxious. At the same time worries trap us in the future and therefore prevent us from bringing attention to the present moment. An affirmation formulated in the present tense allows us to detach from our past and future Self and move into the present moment. Use the affirmations students share to put together a list to close the retreat. I invited students to repeat these either quietly in their head or to say them out loud with me.

> I am worthy.
> I always have more than enough.
> I am perfect just as I am.
> I accept who I am. It is safe for me to be myself.
> I love the way I look and feel. My body is beautiful.
> Loving myself allows me to give more to others.
> I release my past and I believe in myself.
> I am good enough.

5.4 'Good Enough': Considerations

The four foundations of mindfulness are carefully built into the retreat structure without conceptually explaining it. This approach can be helpful if you are not certain about the student's relationship to mindfulness and any preconceptions that would hinder them joining and fully engaging. Using terminology that lands with students is a suitable workaround. You might find that students are interested to learn more about the mindfulness principles underpinning the retreat and are keen to access resources. I usually have a list of different resources available for them, which I share via email after the retreat so that they can dive deeper into their personal exploration journey. I use a combination of my own materials, books, YouTube videos, and podcasts.

Although this session was a one-off extracurricular activity, its impact can be wide reaching. For some students this was the first time that they had participated in such a session. The concepts and the way of connecting to self were new to them. For others, it was familiar territory, and they found the session helpful to strengthen their relationship with themselves and in some cases rekindle a regular practice. What this retreat emphasises is that to become a leader it is okay to reflect and to take time to look inside, especially now there are more and more business students who are not afraid to be vulnerable and to share their battle with mental health openly. However, not all students who struggle are ready to open up. A retreat like this allows them to collectively explore shared beliefs and experiences, which in turn cultivates a sense of compassion for themselves and others, which is a valuable leadership skill (Boyatzis et al., 2006; Martin & Heineberg, 2017). Leadership is about people, and therefore effective leaders must have compassion not just high performance orientation (Brodbeck et al., 2002). Leaders who experience compassion for themselves and others through retreats like this, including opportunities for reflection, have reported psychophysiological benefits which enabled them to be more sustainable as leaders (Boyatzis et al., 2006).

Chapter 5 in a nutshell...

Do not make assumptions about what business students need or would like to develop leadership skills. Instead co-create extracurricular mindfulness sessions with students, and give students agency over their 'extra' learning. Refrain from give any sense that you know what is best or that you are doing your students a favour. Any mindfulness sessions should be focused on the students participating and how the tools used can benefit their wellbeing and connection to Self with the purpose of becoming self-aware future leaders.

It might sound harsh, but you are not the centre of attention: the students are. Such sessions are not about transmitting expertise and knowledge about mindfulness theory. The goal is to provide a space for exploration and for learning about themselves. As mindfulness teachers and facilitators, we become servants to the pursuit of developing future leaders. Being able to guide students to discover their own worth and internalise a feeling of being good enough is one step in the right direction. Being a mindful future leader is not as much about how they will interact, collaborate with, and treat others as it is about learning to understand themselves and to manage themselves in a way that is mindful. Only then can they lead others with kindness, love, and compassion in a genuine and authentic way.

While a one-off event might not result in a tidal wave, do not underestimate its impact beyond the people in the room. In 2024, I almost had to cancel the retreat due to other commitments, but the society was adamant about it taking place, and the society wrote me an email:

> Your session was so well received over the years, that I would hate to miss the opportunity to book you and give our students the opportunity ... everyone was raving about it and said that it got them through some dark times.

A one-off event is a starting point, and it can ignite many lights beyond what we can see. I would like to close this chapter with the following quote from the Buddha, who famously said: '*Our life is shaped by our mind: we become what we think.*' (Goodreads, n.d.)

References

Arranz, N., Ubierna, F., Arroyabe, M. F., Perez, C., & Fdez. de Arroyabe, J. (2017). The effect of curricular and extracurricular activities on university students' entrepreneurial intention and competences. *Studies in Higher Education*, 42(11), 1979–2008.

Bartkus, K. R., Nemelka, B., Nemelka, M., & Gardner, P. (2012). Clarifying the meaning of extracurricular activity: A literature review of definitions. *American Journal of Business Education (AJBE)*, 5(6), 693–704.

Boone, L. E., Kurtz, D. L., & Fleenor, C. P. (1988). CEOs: Early signs of a business career. *Business Horizons*, 31(5), 20–24.

Boyatzis, R. E., Smith, M. L., & Blaize, N. (2006). Developing sustainable leaders through coaching and compassion. *Academy of Management Learning & Education*, 5(1), 8–24.

Brewer, J. A., & Roy, A. (2021). Can approaching anxiety like a habit lead to novel treatments? *American Journal of Lifestyle Medicine*, 15(5), 489–494.

Brewer, J. A., Roy, A., Deluty, A., Liu, T., & Hoge, E. A. (2020). Can mindfulness mechanistically target worry to improve sleep disturbances? Theory and study protocol for app-based anxiety program. *Health Psychology*, 39(9), 776–784.

Brodbeck, F. C., Frese, M., & Javidan, M. (2002). Leadership made in Germany: Low on compassion, high on performance. *Academy of Management Perspectives*, 16(1), 16–29.

Goldstein, J. (2013). *Mindfulness: A practical guide to awakening*. Sounds True.

Goodreads. (n.d.). *Quote by Gautama Buddha*. Retrieved August 2. 2024, from https://www.goodreads.com/quotes/3221781-our-life-is-shaped-by-our-mind-for-we-become.

Herzberg, F. (2017). *Motivation to work*. Routledge.

Hitchcock, S., Seno-Alday, S., & Chandra, P. (2024). Missing the mark: Lessons from failing to foster learner engagement in a co-curricular program. *Journal of Management Education*. https://doi.org/10.1177/10525629241249764.

Isopahkala-Bouret, U., Siivonen, P., & Haltia, N. (2023). 'Some people may feel socially excluded and distressed': Finnish business students' participation in extracurricular activities and the accumulation of cultural capital. *Journal of Education and Work*, 36(1), 52–64.

Martin, D., & Heineberg, Y. (2017). Positive leadership, power and compassion. In P. Gilbert, (Ed.), *Compassion* (pp. 221–236). Routledge.

Perrakis, A. (2018). *The ultimate guide to chakras: The beginners guide to balancing, healing and unblocking your chakras for health and positive energy*. Fair Winds Press.

Skinner, B. F. (1971). Operant conditioning. *The Encyclopedia of Education*, 7, 29–33.

6
EMBEDDING MINDFULNESS AT PROGRAMME/COURSE LEVEL

6.1 Personal and professional development streams

An alternative to extra-curricular activities is to embed mindfulness as part of a personal and professional stream alongside the programme structure – one that ties in strategically with the programme learning outcomes and provides students with an opportunity to expand learning beyond subject-specific modules but that has deep personal relevance. Embedding a personal and professional development stream as part of the programme can be done in two ways.

One option is to create credit-bearing modules in each academic year or semester throughout the whole programme, with a mindfulness component or focus as part of professional skills development, that are aligned with an employability agenda. Each module might have summative assessments that assess students' knowledge and transferable skills around mindfulness and employability for instance. Reflective podcasts are a great vehicle to measure such learning outcomes. At Surrey Business School, we have integrated mindfulness into our employability stream and offer a credit-bearing module in each year of study (first year to final year). This works well at undergraduate level due to the length and scheduling of modules over a longer period. Chapter 7 will dive deeper into embedding mindfulness at module level for undergraduate students.

In contrast, the shorter and more compact nature of postgraduate programmes makes them less suitable for such an approach. Another option is to design a personal and professional development stream that is still strategically part of the programme but is unassessed and that can be used as a unique selling point to attract students. The stream becomes a differentiator for the programme, while at the same time, emphasising a value-added aspect for individuals. Applicants like a personalised and bespoke component that enriches their experience while studying, and even more so if it has a positive impact beyond their degree. This approach also aligns with postgraduate students' motivations to further their education or obtain another degree, which is usually intrinsically driven. At the same time, advertising a personal element as part of the study experience taps into the desire of getting more than knowledge; it becomes experiential from the start.

MBA cohorts are probably the most studied group of people in business school environments in relation to personal and professional development streams that sit alongside the programme structure and in the context of practicing mindfulness. MBA students are an accessible group of students with an interesting dynamic of characteristics, which makes them suitable and receptive for mindfulness practices to be explored (Asthana, 2021; Krishnan, 2021; Sadler-Smith & Shefy, 2007). They are eager to learn about themselves and to transform from where they are now to something that is bigger, more profound, and includes transformation of Self.

If I wanted to paint a picture of a typical MBA student based on my experience and literature, I would describe MBA students as driven, eager to learn, competitive, and goal-oriented. At times, they might appear over-confident with a flavour of superior in comparison to regular master's course students with the ultimate dream of become a C-Suite leader after graduation or the next Elon Musk. I appreciate that this description is clichéd and judgmental, and I can say with certainty that this picture does not represent every MBA student, yet MBA students are aware of the label, which in turn puts enormous pressure on MBA students and how they become. Increased stress, fear, worry, and self-doubt, which in mindfulness are hindrances to contentment, are the result. Neither the label nor the associated emotional concepts are helpful for anyone, and they are certainly not for people who aspire to become future leaders. MBA providers recognise the dichotomy and have added much needed professional development streams to their programmes to address this issue with a focus on future career development. Since my time as MBA Director, I have seen investment and a trend towards providing MBA students with more personal development to support their learning journey as well as their future aspirations. Mindfulness workshops are on the rise in MBA classrooms. This trend has also been fuelled by CEOs sharing success stories rooted in daily meditation practices and working with mindfulness coaches (Roche et al., 2014). The number one mindfulness tool CEOs share is the use of meditation to enhance resilience, emotional intelligence, enhance creativity and improve relationships (Seppälä, 2017).

6.2 'Enrich Your Study Life': Case study

Developing self-aware future leaders starts in the classroom. As we have established already, co-creation and relevance drive engagement and commitment. The aim of 'Enrich your Study Life' is to offer MBA students a space to access inner resources to support their learning journey and to cultivate inner wisdom to serve their future goals as leaders. In collaboration with students and academics and based on my experience as a mindfulness coach, I developed five workshops to guide this journey. Ideally, workshops are scheduled over five consecutive weeks. In our case, we had to spread them out over 15 weeks. In addition to the in-person workshops, students had access to an online space to continue self-paced learning and practice. Resources for each workshop are below.

Each workshop was scheduled for two hours and focused on a particular foundation of mindfulness contextualised to students' study life. The first workshop, called 'Body, Intention, and Breath,' relates to the first foundation of mindfulness, mindfulness of the body. The second workshop, 'Feelings and Self-Awareness,' covers the second foundation of mindfulness, mindfulness of feeling tone. The third workshop, 'Mind and Self-Acceptance,' refers to the third foundation of mindfulness, mindfulness of the mind. The fourth workshop, 'Hindrances and Manifestation' reflects elements of the four foundations of mindfulness, mindfulness of *Dharma*. I deliberately used terminology that was relevant to students' study life and the idea of enrichment. Conversations were rich and immensely rewarding for both me, as the facilitator, and the participants. The final workshop, which was held as a coaching space, enabled students to dive deep into their inner wisdom and it was humbling to experience transformation taking place.

6.3 'Enrich Your Study Life': Resources

Workshop 1: Body, intention, and breathing

Moving from expectations to intentions

The first workshop was centred around the first foundation of mindfulness, mindfulness of the body. I invited students to first share their intention for choosing the MBA course and their expectations and worries related to their study journey before moving into how this journey of studying is experienced somatically. To capture intention, expectations, and worries, you can use Post-it notes that can be placed on a table or wall. Displaying students' thoughts demonstrates the collective experience and provides an entrance into the conversation around the value of *good* intentions, the impact of expectations, and the role of worries. Expectations and worries are interlinked, both can have a negative impact on our experience if we cling to them. Both draw out attention away from the present moment into the future, which creates tension in our mind and our body. I refer to expectations as absolute constructs, unchangeable, unmoveable. Because of their almost fixed nature, expectations result in worrying about meeting them. If we rephrase an expectation as an intention, we remove that absoluteness and instil flexibility, which enables students to open their mind and body up to possibility. Before moving into intention setting, it is helpful to give space to worries and how the body feels right now.

Ask students again to share, on a Post-it note, their experience about how they feel right now. Create another space for the comments and group them in clusters. The most used words in these sessions are stressed, anxious, under pressure, and doubt. Continue the exploration by asking if they experience any tension in the body and where. The areas that are most referred to are head, shoulders, and chest. This is a great starting point to invite students to participate in a breathing exercise to learn to focus their attention, in this case on the breath, followed by a body scan to loosen the tension and give them access to their awareness intelligence, which will enable students to become mindful with themselves in the process. You can either let breath work flow into the body scan or practise them separately and invite students to write down experiences in between. The latter can be helpful to break the experience up and allow space for reflection. I find that this works well with students who are new to mindfulness practices. While you are guiding students through the process speak slowly and take a couple of breaths in-between instructions, so that students have time to feel the meditation settle in.

Meditation: 15 minutes – The breath as focus of attention

Sit comfortably on your chair and place your hands on your thighs or knees. Place both feet on the ground. You can take your shoes off if that feels good. Start to bring your attention to the connection between feet and the floor. Feel the weight of the feet on the ground. Now bring your attention to the hands on your thighs or knees. Feel the connection between your hands and your legs.

With your next inhale, lengthen through the spine, and as you exhale, allow your shoulders to drop. Feel the weight of the elbows and hands resting on your legs. Let us do this one more time. Breathe in through the nose or mouth, lengthen through the spine, and exhale let go of the shoulders.

Bring your attention to the breath, your inhale and your exhale.

As you breathe in, feel the temperature of the air touching the back of your throat, and notice the temperature of your aim as you exhale.

With your next inhale, become aware of the sound of your breath. Maybe you are familiar with the sound of your breath; maybe you are new to it.

Bring your attention to where you are breathing into the body. Are you breathing into the belly or the chest? Can you feel your whole body moving as you breathe?

What sensations do you notice as you breathe? Is there tightness, spaciousness in the body?

Finally, bring your attention back to the inhale and exhale. What is the length of your inhale?

What is the length of your exhale? Do you notice the little pause between inhale and exhale?

We are going to lengthen our inhale and exhale so we can deepen our connection and keep our focus on the breath. We will breathe in for the count of three and out for the count of three, in for four and out for four, all the way to eight, and then we reverse.

Let us begin. Breathe in for three, two, one. Hold. Exhale three, two, one.

Inhale for four, three, two, one. Hold, Exhale for four three, two, one.

Inhale for five, four, three, two, one. Hold. Exhale for five, four three, two, one.

Inhale for six, five, four, three, two, one. Hold. Exhale for six, five, four three, two, one.

Inhale for seven, six, five, four, three, two, one. Hold. Exhale for seven, six, five, four three, two, one.

Inhale for eight, seven, six, five, four, three, two, one. Hold. Exhale for eight, seven, six, five, four three, two, one.

Inhale for seven ... Exhale for seven.

Inhale for six... Exhale for six.

Inhale for five ... Exhale for five.

Inhale for four ... Exhale for four.

Inhale for three ... Exhale for three. Return to your normal rhythm of breath. Bring your attention to how you feel. How the body feels, how the mind feels. [You can lead into a body scan here or take a short break.]

Allow students to remain in stillness and silence for two minutes. Then gently bring them back into the room, invite them to open their eyes and to write down anything that has arisen during the practice.

Meditation: 20 minutes – Body scan: Permission to let go

As you are sitting on your chair, bring your attention to your forehead. Relax the muscles in your face; relax the muscles around your eyes, cheeks, and jaw. Maybe open your mouth slightly and let the tongue hang. Relax the muscles in your throat and your neck.

With your next breath in, let go of tension in your shoulders and bring your attention to your left arm. Relax the muscles in your left upper arm, elbow, and forearm. Let go of tension in your wrist, the palm of your left hand and fingers. With every exhale feel the weight of your left arm, heavy and relaxed.

Bring your attention to right shoulder. Let go of tension in your right shoulder. Relax the muscles in your right upper arm, elbow, and forearm. Let go of tension in your wrist, the palm of your right hand and fingers. With every exhale feel the weight of your right arm, heavy and relaxed.

Come back to your breath. Notice the chest and belly rising and falling as you breathe in and out. Feel the muscles in your chest and belly soften, relax.

Bring your attention to your left hip. Let go of tension in your left hip. Relax the muscles in your left thigh, knee, and calf. Let go of tension in your left ankle, foot, and toes. With every breath you let go of tension in your leg.

> Bring your attention to your right hip. Let go of tension in your right hip. Relax the muscles in your right thigh, knee, and calf. Let go of tension in your right ankle, foot and toes. With every breath you let go of tension in your leg.
>
> With your next inhale, imagine you are breathing in a white light. This light travels up to your head and fills your head, softens your tissue and skin. With your next exhale, observe the light travel down into your throat, shoulders, and arms. It is a warm, gentle light. With every exhale, you breathe the light more into the body, and you watch it fill your torso, your hip space and travel down your legs into your feet. Keep breathing it into and through the body, and watch it as it disappears into the ground. Let go of worries, expectations, stress, and anxiety. Watch the light until it is all gone. You feel relaxed, supported, and safe. You are here in the present moment. Stillness and silence settle in.

Gently bring students back into the room and give them time to reflect on their experience. Once students have had time to reflect you can invite them to share their experience. You might be surprised that this is often the first time that students have participated in a body scan and so it can be a profound somatic experience. Now they know how it feels to relax, to let go, and they know that they can access that state. It is a good time to invite them to return to intentions.

Coaching: Creating good intentions

A good intention is specific and focuses on a process rather than an outcome. An expectation to submit assignments on time and to aim for an A* for instance is difficult to embody. It mainly resides as an absolute construct in the mind. The attention also resides on the outcome rather than the process of doing the assignment, which means that the student is removed from the present moment and therefore the ability to focus. The good intention would be to put attention on the ability to focus and concentrate on one specific assessment at a time. If students are due to submit multiple assessments, for instance, a good intention would be one such as: I dedicate focus time to each of my assessments. The intention needs to be formulated in the present tense. From this place, encourage students to go deeper by asking, 'What do you need to dedicate focus time to each assessment?'

After the two exercises you might bring the conversation back to some science around breathing and the importance of breathing through the nose. James Nestor's book (Nestor, 2020) *Breath* is very helpful to provide further information.

Journaling

The final part of this first workshop looks at the act of journaling (Elsey, 2021; Wolfenden, 2020). Some students might be familiar with this and already journal, whereas for others it might be new. I set them the homework to give it a go and purchase a journal that speak to them. Journaling is used by entrepreneurs and CEOs. I usually share insights from my own practice with clients outside academia. Journaling has been found to be not just a transformational coaching tool (Elsey, 2021) but a tool to create space for thoughts and paying attention to thoughts and feelings and allowing these to be externalised. Bell, one the MBA students in 2023, described the value of journaling like this:

> I might feel really stressed about an assignment and go for a walk and focus on my breath. When I come back home, I write everything down, and I feel like I have organised the mess in my head because I can look objectively at what is going on. It allows me to detach and observe the thoughts from a distance, and I can move on.
>
> *Bell, 23–24, MBA student*

Journaling is a very personal activity, and it can be helpful to try out different approaches to journaling. I recommend using the journal not just as a dumping ground for negative, painful thoughts but as a *safe* space to explore and to reflect. Finish an entry with an affirmation and potential intention, this is particularly useful when exploration has uncovered unpleasantness or has led to feeling upset or sad. For me a journal is a place of honesty, being truthful with myself. I let my thoughts and emotions flow. Sometimes there are more of these than other days, and sometimes I don't feel like committing these to the page. Gratitude journals are another option for students to explore. Personally, I found gratitude journals less explorative and helpful for my own journey.

Workshop 2: Feelings and self-awareness

The second workshop builds on the knowledge of the first workshop and leads from the first foundation of mindfulness, mindfulness of the body, to the second foundation of mindfulness, mindfulness of feeling tone. We utilise the insights gained about our connection to body, breath, and mind to go deeper into understanding ourselves and how we can use those insights to enrich study life. The workshop explores our world of feelings and how understanding feelings better helps develop more internal and external self-awareness (Goleman et al., 2018).

Feeling tone is concerned with what we experience, perceive, and feel as either pleasant or unpleasant or neutral. Naturally, humans enjoy the experience of pleasant feelings, and we gravitate towards that because our inner being seeks pleasantness and contentment. Hence, we often experience imbalance. We use the expression *feeling out of sorts*. Most of us can sense being out of sorts, but it is a lot harder to understand and move the dial. We explored the following questions and concepts in relation to the second foundation of mindfulness:

- How can we move from unpleasant to pleasant feeling tones and do we want that? Is change always desired?
- How can we also appreciate neutrality?
- What concepts underpin our understanding and move to change?

The workshop was guided by three exercises, chocolate meditation, alternate nostril breathing, and smile mediation to explore the feeling tones of pleasantness, unpleasantness, and neutrality in different ways and highlight how we can become more mindful during study days that are stressful, which are usually perceived as unpleasant. Below are scripts for chocolate and smile meditation. For alternate nostril breathing I recommend the book *The Healing Breath* by Jack Angelo (2010). The author refers to alternate nostril beathing as balancing breath (Angelo, 2010, pp. 69–70).

Students are particularly drawn to the idea of chocolate meditation, and I have rarely encountered someone who was not happy to participate. If, however, chocolate is not suitable for a student, you can use a raisin instead. I use dark chocolate because it is richer in smell and taste. Make sure you also have a vegan version, so you accommodate for any allergies. Vegan chocolate is usually gluten and dairy free. Break the chocolate into a number of raisin-sized pieces. Below is a script you can use to facilitate this meditation.

Chocolate meditation: Ten minutes

> Find a comfortable seat, and turn your right-hand palm facing. I will place a small piece of chocolate in your palm. Leave it there and look at it.
> Focus your gaze on the piece of chocolate.
>
> - What do you see?
> - Does the chocolate have a particular shape?
> - Does it remind you of something?
> - What is the texture like?
> - Are the edges round or sharp?
> - Can you feel the weight of the piece of chocolate on your hand? Is the chocolate changing, melting?
> - Can you smell the chocolate?
> - How does your mouth respond?
> - How does your mind respond? Is contemplation of the piece of chocolate pleasant, unpleasant, or neutral?
>
> Keep your focus on the chocolate, and take a long deep breath in, and gently let that go. Let us do this one more time. Take a long deep breath in, and release.
> Now, place your piece of chocolate on your tongue, and notice what happens. Close your eyes, and sit with the experience, the sensation in the mouth,

in the body. Are there thoughts or emotions arising. Is the experience pleasant, unpleasant, or neutral?

When the chocolate is completely melted and the taste is fading, open your eyes, and bring your attention back to the room. Write down anything that has arisen for you. What was pleasant, what was unpleasant, what was neutral about this experience? What do you know about yourself now that you did not know ten minutes ago?

After the meditation

Invite students to share their experiences and ask them what thoughts arose and how these relate to their experience of studying. Common themes that students share are that sometimes we want to get to our goal quickly, and we do not take the time to fully immerse ourselves in the process. Whether this relates to always thinking about the assessment outcome while working on the assessment or thinking already of the jobs and salary we want after completion of the programme. Give space for exploration and insights to develop. Another topic that students discuss is the concept of impermanence. Similar to the chocolate disappearing after a while, students recognise that situations change, and even if we experience something very unpleasant, it will pass.

This meditation feeds nicely into a conversation about self-awareness and what it requires to become self-aware, to learn to know your Self. Smile meditation is well suited to starting the conversation about self-awareness.

Smile meditation: Ten minutes

>Sit comfortably with your feet flat on the ground. Place your hands on your thighs or on your knees. Feel the connection of the feet on the ground. Feel the connection of the sit bones on the chair. Take a long deep breath in, and lengthen through the spine. As you exhale, drop the shoulders and relax the body, but maintain a long, straight spine. Take a couple of breaths in and out. You can keep your eyes open or closed.
>
>Bring your attention to your face. Relax the muscles in your face, on your forehead, around your eyes, cheeks, and jaw. Notice how it feels. Notice the shape of your mouth.
>
>With your next breath in, start to smile, and allow your smile to become bigger and bigger, so much so that you have to open your mouth and you have to physically pull the corners of the mouth towards your ears. Keep that smile there. We hold the smile for about two minutes. This is a conscious effort. Notice how it feels. Maybe it is pleasant, maybe unpleasant, maybe neutral. Maybe you feel silly or wonder what others think. Notice what thoughts arise, and be okay with them.
>
>Gently release the exorbitant smile by closing your mouth but keeping the smile still. Hold it for two minutes again. Notice how it changes your feelings,

your thoughts. Become aware of how your feeling tone shifts. Does it feel more pleasant or less so?

Gently release the smile and allow your mouth, your lips to soften to relax. If you have not closed your eyes already, now is a good time to go deeper. We stay here for about three minutes. Become aware of how you feel now. Are you still concerned about how it looks? What others think? What has changed?

When you are ready, open your eyes, and bring your attention back into the room. Maybe write down any thoughts and feelings that have arisen for you.

After the meditation, I lead students into a short lecture about the concept of self-awareness in the context of feeling tone. Self-awareness research distinguishes between internal and external self-awareness (Eurich, 2018). Internal self-awareness is knowing how you perceive yourself, whereas external self-awareness is knowing how others perceive you. Both are equally important, but we often lack one or the other. It is more likely to have a good sense of internal self-awareness than external self-awareness because it is a lot harder to learn and know how others perceive us. Sometimes we do not want to hear it. We take it personally because it is like holding up a mirror to things we perhaps do not even like about ourselves. On the other hand, it can be helpful to be open to such information because it could also be positive and supportive for our own development. During smile meditation students often report that the exorbitant smile made them feel uncomfortable. It was unpleasant, and they had to keep their eyes open. They look at how others react, and they maybe even stop because they struggle to stay in that state. Only when they closed their eyes were they able to let go of that and focus on their internal awareness. In contrast, the normal smile makes students feel good about themselves. Those who have their eyes open feel welcomed in the group. Students experience pleasantness, and they are perceived as *happy* too. As homework, I ask students to pay attention to their internal and external self-awareness, particularly in group work tasks, and to ask peers who they feel comfortable with for feedback. A greater sense of self-awareness leads to greater self-acceptance.

Workshop 3: Mind and self-acceptance

While thoughts were explored in the first two workshops, until this point little attention has been given to the mind and what and where the *mind* is or the relationship we hold with the mind. I like to start this workshop by asking students where they believe their mind is or exists in the body and what makes them think that it has a particular location. Some explain that they believe the mind is in the head. Conceptually our mind is associated with our head and more specifically with our brain space. Therefore, it is natural to assume that. Others believe the mind is in the heart or even the whole body (Blake, 2009). Following on, I ask students to describe their state of mind at this moment. This conversation leads nicely into the types of minds we can experience, in particular the contracted/constricted mind and the distracted mind and how to obtain a quiet mind.

Contracted mind

A contracted mind, also known as a constricted mind, experiences a lack of physical and mental energy. This is referred to as sloth (physical lack of energy) and torpor (mental lack of energy), which we touched upon in the first chapter. A mind that is contracted feels tight, anxious. It might be filled with greed due to a scarcity mindset trapping the person in the contracted mind state. A way to shift from a contracted mind and clear lack of energy would be to practice generosity. Equally a mind that is filled with desire to perform at the highest level struggles and needs to learn to let go of the outcome to feel less contracted. The following meditation supports students to practise letting go and move from a contracted to an empty mind so they can cultivate a new state of mind. We practise a short meditation where we use the word empty to clear our mind from sloth and torpor.

Empty meditation: Five minutes

> Find a comfortable seat, either on a chair or cushion, or you can lie down. Bring your attention to the connection between the chair or cushion and your sit bones. Notice your hands gently resting in your knees or thighs. Direct your attention to the breath. Notice your inhale and exhale. With your next inhale, lengthen through the spine, and with your next exhale, drop the shoulders. Practice that a couple of times.
>
> When you feel like you have settled in, start to repeat the word *empty*. You can say it out loud, or you can repeat it quietly in your head. Repeat it for approximately three minutes. You can set yourself a timer. When you have finished repeating the word *empty*, sit there in stillness and silence, and bring your attention to your mind. Observe it. If you still feel that your thoughts are returning to previous ones, then repeat the word again and add *I let go*. With every exhale imagine you are letting your thoughts drift away. When you are ready, open your eyes, and take a moment to write down anything that has arisen for you.

Distracted mind

In contrast, a distracted mind might feel like a thousand thoughts enter the mind, which we can experience as feeling unable to organise thoughts. Each thought turns into the next and the next and the next, until an outside noise or stimuli takes attention away. This is a typical scenario students share while studying, along with the desperation that comes with it, which they cling onto to remain focused.

One student shared that he feels like he is sometimes slightly addicted to being distracted, especially while preparing for assessments. He explained that he would feel the need to tirelessly scroll through his phone, checking messages or read receipts. Yet, at the same time, he worried and felt guilty about not focusing on the assessment and ruminated on the fact that he might not be able to get the grades he wants. Being able to change our state of mind from feeling distracted to focused requires practice and understanding about what an undistracted mind looks like conceptually, what it feels like, and what would help to remind us of that.

Exercise: 30 minutes – What would an undistracted mind look and feel like?

> Split a piece of paper in the middle and draw a line. On the left side write down anything that distracts you at present and add the emotions and sensations that come with it. On the right side write down how it would feel if you were undistracted. What emotions and sensations would be helpful?

When students are finished, invite them to practice the following meditation that can help them to move from a distracted to a quiet mind. Along this path students learn to accept what they are experiencing as distracting without attaching to it, without following the urge and craving for distraction. The following mediation can be a useful tool to practise that. It is also available on YouTube (TEDx Talks, 2022). I delivered this meditation as part of a TEDx talk series at the University of Surrey in May 2022.

Quiet your mind meditation: 15 minutes

> Find a comfortable seat, on a chair or a cushion. Place your hands on your thighs. Focus your attention on the connection between the feet and the floor, the sit bones and the chair or cushion. Feel your hands on your thighs. Notice your belly, your chest move as you inhale and exhale. How does your body feel, how does your mind feel? [Instructor leaves time for space.]
>
> Maybe your mind is busy. Thoughts moving about at speed. Like rockets shooting into the air. Maybe there is a sensation of restlessness and business. Accept that for a moment and observe it. [Instructor leaves time for space.]
>
> With your next inhale, imagine you are breathing in white energy. Observe how the energy enters your nostrils and touches the back of your throat. With every inhale, you breathe more white energy into the body. The energy travels up into your head and into the shoulders, arms, heart space, and hips. You can feel your body being nourished and cleansed of any thoughts that no longer serve you. Your mind feels calm and quiet. You keep breathing in the white energy, and it starts to go beyond your physical form. It surrounds you, covers you. All you can see is a white space around you. You are rested and calm. There is a feeling of peacefulness and clarity. All is quiet. Your mind is quiet. Your body is quiet. Take some time and sit with the sensation, accept what you

experience. Feel the spaciousness within you and around you. [Instructor leaves plenty of time to experience either in silence or using the paragraph below to guide, three minutes.]

Give students the opportunity to journal and write down whatever has arisen.

You might notice that sustaining attention comes and goes. We all experience meditation in a different way. It takes practice, but it is all right and good. Throughout this process of noticing, observing, and feeling what is, become accepting of your experience. Become comfortable with the experience in the present moment. You might notice that raging over what is only results in a contracted and distracted mind, which is not helpful in moving forwards. Accept your experience. [Give space to accept.]

Gently bring your awareness to your exhale. With every exhale the white energy surrounding you becomes less dense. Observe it until it disappears. Bring your attention back to your feet and toes, to your hands and fingers. Maybe move or stretch, and open your eyes if that feels good.

The process of becoming comfortable with what is arising in meditation is a powerful way to learn acceptance of what is and the role of the Self within that. The ability to access and use awareness in such a way allows us to understand and see from a distance how the mind gets tangled in stories and carried away by thoughts. At the same time cultivation of awareness in the present moment enables us to learn to be content with the feelings and experiences that arise and manifest themselves as contraction and distraction often beyond the mind. We notice tension, sensations in certain areas related to unpleasant experiences for instance. The whole body communicates through these channels. Self-acceptance is the process of becoming and feeling okay with what is. Okay in the sense of a neutral feeling tone towards contentment.

Workshop 4: Hindrances and manifestation

It is easy to say *Learn to be okay with what is* and you will accept yourself; it is a lot harder to internalise because along this journey of acceptance are obstacles, which in mindfulness literature are referred to as the five hindrances: desire, aversion, sloth and torpor, restlessness, and worry and doubt. Throughout life, we have learned to cling on to these hindrances either emotionally, mentally, or physically. Sometimes we even seem to experience the opposite of what we want. The workshop starts by exploring questions related to hindrances.

Coaching questions: 20 minutes

- What holds me back? What are obstacles I am aware of at the moment?
- What are my *hindrances* on my current journey and going forwards?
- How can I manifest my new life as a future leader?

In this context students learn about mindfulness of *Dharma*. *Dharma* has many meanings, such as truth or reality (Goldstein, 2013). The definition I prefer to use is the 'truthful' experience and the recognition of the hindrances that affect our experience to live truthfully, 'happily,' contentedly, and mindfully at all times. Students can work through the questions individually, in pairs, or in small groups. Twenty minutes is a good amount of time to go deeper into each hindrance. I invite students to draw their answers for each question on a separate sheet of paper (A3 preferably) and to use different colours. It allows students to zoom out of their experience and detach, which in turn enables them to identify where they are clinging on and whether it might be beneficial to let go. This session can become very dynamic, and students share personal stories and thoughts and how they feel about situations.

Group work has come to be an obstacle for some MBA students. Sometimes the dynamic of a group and how group members take on specific roles can put pressure on students and affect motivation and therefore contribution. Students describe it as feeling less motivated and feeling lethargic about meeting with the group. Lena said: '*I feel tired just thinking about it. They do not listen to me. I might just not be there.*' Lena developed an aversion to working with the others on the assessment and experiences sloth and torpor, which results in non-engagement. Interestingly, some of the other group members were unaware of Lena's experience. Instead, they believed that she could not be bothered, that she was a freeloader. In the workshop, Lena shared that she never put her hand up and put herself forwards in school because she felt incapable of speaking her mind in the presence of others. She was perceived as the quiet one that does the work and never complains. Inside though, she had a desire to speak, to contribute, and to play a role.

To help Lena and other students to work through hindrances, I invited them to join a Sutra meditation. Sutra means stitching two things together. In this case the stitching consists of three aspects, which I share with students as initial coaching questions before going into meditation.

Sutra coaching questions: Ten minutes

1. Is there something in my study life I want to change? Is there something in my study life I want to have more of or less of?
2. Who is related to what I want to change? Just me or someone else?
3. How can I be more ….?

After the students have written down the questions, ask them to share the final question. I usually hand out Post-it notes to write them down, and then I collect them. You might find that there are similar ones, and that is normal and okay. Below are some common questions:

How can I be more patient?
How can I be more compassionate?
How can I let go of the outcome?
How can I be less judgemental?
How can I be more self-loving?

Once you have collected the questions from students, turn them into *I am ...* statements with the students and finally derive nouns to deepen the connection.

Sutra meditation: 20 minutes

Find a comfortable seat on a chair or a cushion. Place your hands on your thighs. Focus your attention on the connection between the feet and the floor, the sit bones and the chair or cushion. Feel your hands on your thighs. Notice your belly, your chest move as you inhale and exhale. How does your body feel, how does your mind feel. [Instructor leaves time for space.]

Bring your attention to the bottom of your belly, where the solar plexus chakra sits. It is called Manipura. Imagine a yellow light. With every inhale, that light gets a little bigger. Keep feeding the light until it is the size of a football. Place your hands in front of your belly; imagine you are holding this energy ball. Feel the subtle sensations in your hands. The solar plexus chakra is the centre for transformation, change, and inner power to make things happen and overcome obstacles. As you feel its warm, comforting energy in your belly area and between your hands, we will ask our questions to initiate change from within. You can say them out loud with me or repeat them quietly in your head. We will repeat them twice, and we will take a long deep breath in and gently let the question go as we exhale. We will sit in stillness for a moment before asking the next question.

How can I be more ....? (repeat twice). Take a long deep breath in, and exhale. Let it go.

If your hands start to feel tired, you can place them on your thighs, palms facing up. Keep your focus in the solar plexus area and on your energy ball. Now, let us affirm what we can change as something that is already happening. We will use *I am* statements. Again, you can say them out loud with me or repeat them quietly in your head. We will repeat them twice and then take a long inhale and gentle exhale to let them go. Let the university sort out the details.

I am .... (repeat twice). Take a long deep breath in, and exhale. Let it go.

TABLE 6.1 Sutra questions and statements

How can I be ...	I am ...	Deepening noun
How can I be more patient?	I am patient.	Patience
How can I be more compassionate?	I am compassionate.	Compassion
How can I let go of the outcome?	I let go of what no longer serves me.	Letting go
How can I be less judgemental?	I am non-judgmental.	Openness
How can I be more self-loving?	I love myself.	Love

Finally, we will take it deeper. Imagine that you are planting the word in the ball itself, imagine it becoming part of you, part of your essence. We will repeat each word five times before moving on to the next one. Let them reside within you. Feel what X feels like. After we have planted the words deep in our body, we will take five minutes of silence.

Noun X .... (Repeat each five times; if some students still have their hands up, guide them to put their hands into their lap.)

[After five minutes] Keep your eyes closed, place your hands on your solar plexus, and notice how you feel. Breathe into the belly, and take three long breaths in and out. Feel your whole body breathing [three breaths]. Gently open your eyes, and take a moment. Maybe write down anything that has arisen for you, or if you wish to stay in meditation for a little longer, do so.

Invite students to share their experiences and what has arisen for them. Sutra meditation is a great way to explore hindrances and let go of clinging, while at the same time manifesting what our inner being really wants and needs to enjoy the study journey and ultimately life. In this meditation students move from a future desire state to experiencing what they desire in the present moment. They feel into it and then anchor it firmly in their consciousness. This figurative anchoring place allows them to come back to it and makes the abstract, sometimes unattainable possible. It has a grounded and calming effect on the nervous and emotional system. Something that was once abstract becomes a more tangible state of being. Students often share later on in coaching sessions that they used this technique during assessment, when they felt stressed and anxious, to calm down and ground themselves. It doesn't have to be or take 20 minutes; it can be done in two if practised regularly.

Workshop 5: One-to-one coaching sessions

The fifth workshop is a dedicated coaching space for students who attended all four workshops beforehand so they can go deeper into their personal and professional development needs as future leaders. Insights, techniques, and transformational stories from these and similar coaching sessions are shared in Chapter 8.

6.4 Consideration for programme/course level integration

Similar to extra-curricular activities, embedding mindfulness approaches at programme/course level requires planning and input from students. Thus, I recommend taking time to conduct consultations with students and even consider testing some approaches before implementing them. Concepts might look great on paper, but the reality might be different. Ask:

- Who are the students participating?
- What are their challenges now? How can you use mindfulness tools to speak to them?

- What additional resources do you need to support students (e.g. technology, online platform)?
- What is the budget?
- Who else would be able to contribute?
- How can you apply the concept in other areas in the business school?
- How can you turn your experience and insights into a scholarly output?

The last two questions emphasise and showcase the value of embedding mindfulness approaches and initiatives and are therefore perceived as worthwhile. You are more likely to get support and buy-in if you can demonstrate that there is wider return on investment.

Chapter 6 in a nutshell...

Embedding mindfulness approaches at programme/course level can be a rewarding and inspiring endeavour. However, it requires planning and commitment from many stakeholders. Start with an intention and make it an invitation for students to contribute. Co-creation is the key.

Be brave, be bold, and trust your intuition. Practise openness and create your own resources to support the journey. Embedding mindfulness in programmes/courses is an art. You need to sharpen the tools and craft transitions and intersections with different topics and areas.

Most importantly practise what you want students to experience. Invite practitioners from industry to share their experiences. Move from transfer of knowledge to learning by doing. Anyone can read how meditation might enhance self-awareness or how breathing techniques support decision making; only the experience in the present moment can unveil its power for the future.

I would like to close Chapter 6 with Verse 12 from *Tao Te Ching*, 'Seek the Spirit,' which one of my students found inspiring and helpful: '*The wise attend to the inner truth and are not fooled by outward appearances. They ignore matter and seek the spirit*' (Tzu, 2021).

References

Angelo, J. (2010). *The healing breath: How to use the power of breathing to heal, reduce stress and improve wellbeing*. Hachette UK.

Asthana, A. N. (2021). Effectiveness of mindfulness in business education: Evidence from a controlled experiment. *International Journal of Management Education*, 19 (2), 100492.

Blake, A. (2009). *Your body is your brain*. Trokay Press.

Elsey, E. L. (2021). Journaling as a transformational coaching tool: 5 powerful journaling exercises for coaches and clients. In L. Monk, & E. Maisel (Eds.), *Transformational Journaling for Coaches, Therapists, and Clients* (pp. 283–288). Routledge.

Eurich, T. (2018). What self-awareness really is (and how to cultivate it). *Harvard Business Review*, 4, 2–8.

Goldstein, J. (2013). *Mindfulness: A practical guide to awakening.* Sounds True.
Goleman, D., Kaplan, R. S., David, S., & Eurich, T. (2018). *Self-awareness* (HBR emotional intelligence series). Harvard Business Press.
Krishnan, H. A. (2021). Mindfulness as a strategy for sustainable competitive advantage. *Business Horizons,* 64(5), 697–709.
Nestor, J. (2020). *Breath: The new science of a lost art.* Penguin.
Roche, M., Haar, J. M., & Luthans, F. (2014). The role of mindfulness and psychological capital on the well-being of leaders. *Journal of Occupational Health Psychology,* 19(4), 476–489.
Sadler-Smith, E., & Shefy, E. (2007). Developing intuitive awareness in management education. *Academy of Management Learning & Education,* 6(2), 186–205.
Seppälä, E. (2017). How meditation benefits CEOs. *Harvard Business Review.*
TEDx Talks. (2022, May 22). *Quiet your Mind and Recharge | Christine Rivers TEDxSurreyUniversity* [Video]. YouTube. https://www.youtube.com/watch?v=mr5urpjaOh8.
Tzu, L. (2021). *Tao Te Ching. The book of the way.* Ancient Renewal.
Wolfenden, S. (2020). Using coaching tools to develop professional practice holistically. *Business Information Review,* 37(3), 111–115.

7
EMBEDDING MINDFULNESS AT MODULE LEVEL AND FOR ASSESSMENT

It might be easy to develop a module called mindfulness for business students, and certainly I believe that such a module should be part of the curriculum (Rubens et al., 2018). However, the term mindfulness, as established in previous chapters, is not a term that is always welcome or embraced with enthusiasm and openness by academics and students alike. Therefore, a module that is concerned with mindfulness or focuses on developing the mindfulness skills of business students might need to be packaged in a way that makes it attractive and meaningful with relevance and applicability to students' future careers (Amoroso & Burke, 2018; Jamison, 2010).

At both undergraduate and postgraduate level, a clear personal and professional development stream as part of a programme with a range of dedicated career and employability modules is best suited to integrate such a module (Gammie et al., 2002; Omar et al., 2015). This allows students to explore mindfulness in the context of career management and potential benefits outside work. Another option would be to offer modules that focus on physical, mental and emotional health as part of wellbeing streams. In business schools this option is less well established and usually builds into personal and professional streams because employability and wellbeing are connected (Gowan, 2012).

In this chapter, I introduce such a module, one that utilises the themes of employability, career management, and wellbeing to share concepts of mindfulness. The module was developed as part of the personal and professional development stream we integrated into our undergraduate business management programmes in 2023, following a university wide curriculum design review. This is the third module offered in the stream and is available to final year students across all business management programmes as an elective.

DOI: 10.4324/9781032637464-11

The module runs over a 12-week semester period and consists of weekly one-hour workshops and two-hour seminar sessions. The workshops focus on practical tools students can learn and apply in their day-to-day study and later working life. A combination of breath work, meditation, journaling, reflection, creative mapping, and coaching structures the workshops. Seminars are intended to explore theory and concepts and work through case studies to expand students' knowledge and understanding of managing their careers in the future.

We called the module 'Managing your Career.' In the module catalogues, students can read the following overview:

The module provides students with knowledge and skills to manage their career(s) successfully and effectively after graduation. Managing your career is as much about professional etiquette as it is about knowing your self. Self-awareness, self-care, resilience, resourcefulness and sustainable ways to navigate turbulent times throughout career(s) are concepts we hear and talk about but rarely learn how to develop and continue developing so that we can manage career(s) successfully. Self-exploration, journaling, introspection, reflection and prospection and sharing of experiences are key techniques used throughout workshops. Workshops are complemented by seminars discussing current research in relation to career management. The assessments deepen knowledge, understanding and further skills development that serves individual career paths in the long term.

While mindfulness is not explicitly mentioned in the description of the module, it underpins the content, assessment, and learning outcomes of the module. The module focuses on eight topics, which can be grouped into three themes, success, self-awareness, and self-care, all of which can be discussed in the context of mindfulness and enabling students to cultivate a mindfulness approach towards managing their career. In consultation with students, alumni, and employers (Rivers & O'Brien, 2019), these three themes were highlighted as most important and of interest to dive deeper into and develop as skills throughout one's career.

7.1 Success and mindfulness for future leaders

Although students often talk about how they have a desire to be successful after graduation, little research has focused on exploring what success means to business students.

Dries (2011) discussed that the concept of career success is often an objectified image of career people, a concept that is rigid and fixed rather than dynamic and changing, and most importantly that it is a social construct. In fact, our definition of and relationship with career success and success in general changes throughout our life. Opening students' minds to the idea that success does not have to be objectified or just linked to performance-related measures enables students to reframe their own definition at a crucial point of their life. The following questions provide a platform to guide students into developing their own definition of success and how to invite different perspectives. Adopting a mindfulness perspective towards success strengthens students' emotional resilience to unexpected events and outcomes (Sauer & Kohls, 2011), which is a useful leadership quality.

Jennings et al. (2013) were interested in understanding the concept of success perceived by business students over four years of study and how the concept changed. By means of Grounded Theory, the authors identified four themes: academic achievement, social and residential success, life management, and academic engagement. Academic achievement was the most common theme. It referred to attaining good grades and improving to attain better grades. Social and residential success included remaining friends with peers after graduation but was most important in the first year. Life management referred to physical, mental, and emotional wellbeing, time management, and attitude to work and became more important to students towards the final year. Academic engagement referred to wanting to learn. However, success and good grades dominate students' understanding of success and desire to learn. Of course, we can explain the former through conditioning and how success is understood in the Western world. The sad truth is that students cling on to that definition, and it can become all-consuming. It is not surprising therefore that performance measures (e.g. grades) result in physical, emotional, and mental suffering. By supporting students to redefine what success means to them and how it might change when they leave university is an important step towards developing mindful future leaders. Developing awareness of different constructs of success can help them to work more collaboratively and understand different work ethics and behaviours.

Page (2016) used a visual and inquiry-based approach (Spronken-Smith & Walker, 2010) to explore the meaning of success with final-year business management students at Bristol Business School, University of the West of England. Thirty-five students participated. Divided into seven groups, each group was tasked with taking five pictures that symbolise success. This visual approach supported an open and inclusive conversation about the concept and construct of success. Pictures included trophies, celebrating students, expensive cars, staircases, and designer shops. The conversations identified different constructs of success, such as material success, competitive success, and the personal qualities needed for success. The latter is particularly of interest as it ties in with mindfulness aspects such as self-motivation, resilience, and goal setting. Responsibility for one's own success arose as a theme that would determine success potential throughout conversations. Inquiry into the concept of success can provide a great starting point for students to identify how their desire of success might affect their physical, mental, and emotional wellbeing and contribute to their suffering as understood in the fourth foundation of mindfulness, *Dharma*.

Connecting success with mindfulness provides students with a different perspective on their career choice. The visual inquiry-based approach used by Page (2016) is certainly a creative method that gives tangibility to the exploration of success and becoming mindful.

Reinforcing the exploration with coaching questions can further support the development of a mindful perspective towards success. I like to start by inviting students to create a vision board or individual concept map of their perception of success. This can help students to learn about themselves and become more self-aware.

Activity: Creating a mindful success concept map (20 minutes)

1. Provide students with a sheet of A3 paper or use an application such as Padlet or Canva. In the centre of the space write the word SUCCESS. First, let students brainstorm and write down anything that comes up. This can take about five minutes (set a time or play music).
2. Ask students to group their words into themes that make sense to them. It could be performance, status, and so on.
3. Ask student to circle the theme that they believe is most important to them.
4. Ask students to circle the theme that they believe would make them happiest. (It might be the same or a different one.)
5. Invite students to share their insights in triads and ask each other the following questions:

    a What makes this theme most important to you?
    b How would you feel if that does not work out?
    c What makes you believe this would make you happy?
    d What could get in the way of your happiness?

The questions encourage students to explore desire and attachment in relation to their concept and construct of success. I use the foundations of mindfulness to go deeper into that exploration and help students understand that success is subjective, culturally constructed, and changes over time and that this highlights distortion of experience and impermanence (Goldstein, 2013). Distortion of experience refers to distortion of perception, mind, and view, which are integral aspects of defining success for ourselves. The example commonly used is that someone is walking in the woods and believes they have seen a snake, but it turns out to be a stick (distortion of perception). The person overthinks the situation and ruminates over the mistake (distortion of mind). Distortion of the mind is the deepest distortion level and the most difficult to defuse. It is characterised by still believing something to be the *truth* despite having evidence that it is not.

7.2 Self-awareness and mindfulness for future leaders

The above exercise leads nicely into exploring self-awareness in more depth and how to bring a mindful perspective to how we perceive ourselves and how we believe we are perceived by others. Diver and Lock (2019) emphasise the need for business students to develop self-awareness knowledge and skills and autonomy to ensure they can manage with increasingly uncertain futures. Goleman (2011) refers in particular to emotional self-awareness as a critical skill for leaders to develop. (Emotional) self-awareness is one of four domains (self-management, social awareness, relationship management) of emotional intelligence but without (emotional) self-awareness the other three domains might not work properly. While we can read and lecture students about the necessity of developing self-awareness, how we support students to develop self-awareness in general is less well documented. Coach supported workshops and reflections are well suited and are practised in business education as a tool to further self-awareness (Lawrence et al., 2018). Both coaching questions and mindfulness tools such as meditation enable students to explore their own knowledge, understanding and relationship of self-awareness as a concept and life tool. Below are two tools to engage students with their own self-awareness of how they perceive themselves and how they believe they are perceived by others and how to use these insights to empathise with peers.

(Emotional) Self-awareness meditation (20 minutes)

> Find a comfortable seat on a chair or on a cushion on the floor. If you are sitting on a chair, gently place your feet on the ground. You can also take your shoes off. Place your hands on your thighs.
>
> With your next inhale, lengthen through the spine, and as you exhale, relax the shoulders, feel the weight of your arms and hands on your legs. Breathe in, grow taller. Breathe out, loosen up a little more.
>
> Gently bring your attention to your breath. Become aware of the temperature of the breath touching the back of your throat as you inhale and the temperature of the air as you exhale.
>
> Notice how it feels in the nose as you inhale. How your nostrils gently inflate and how it feels in the body as you exhale. Maybe you can hear the sound of your breath. Maybe that sound is new to you; maybe you are familiar with the sound.
>
> Keep your awareness on the breath. Watch it go in and out. Observe the breath flowing without force, just happening. [Instructor: give space for students to experience that for about 10–20 breaths.]
>
> Gently bring your attention to how you are feeling in this moment. Maybe there is some restlessness; maybe thoughts come and go; maybe you already feel calm.
>
> Bring your attention to any physical sensations in your arms, hands, and fingers. [Leave space for awareness to settle in.]
>
> Bring your attention to any physical sensations in your legs, feet, and toes. [Leave space for awareness to settle in.]

Bring your attention to any physical sensations in your belly and chest and back. [Leave space for awareness to settle in.]

Allow the body and mind to relax, to loosen up. Keep your awareness on what arises within you. Noticing without judging. Observing with kindness. What is your state of mind now? How does the body feel? What emotions are you experiencing? Sit for a moment and take your time to be aware of the experience of the present moment until you hear the sound of the chimes/my voice, and if you drift off, come back to the breath, centre your awareness. [3–5 min silence]

When you are ready, come back into the room. Take any movement that feels good, sigh it out and write down anything that has arisen for you. [Give five minutes for people to journal or take a comfort break.]

Self-awareness recall – Coaching questions, journaling, and reflection (30 minutes)

After meditation guide students to go deeper into exploration of their self-awareness.

Recall 1: Remember a situation at work or in a study group where you felt uncomfortable working with someone.

- What made that situation uncomfortable for you?
- Where in the body did you feel discomfort?
- Did you share your experience with everyone? If yes, what was the response? If no, why not?
- What strategies did you use to ease the discomfort?
- How successful were these?
- What would you do if you were in the situation again?
- How do you think the other(s) experienced that situation? How do you know?
- Whatever led to the discomfort, how much empathy did you have at the time with others involved in the same situation? Elaborate on your insight.

Recall 2: Remember a situation at work or in a study group where you felt comfortable working with someone.

- What made that situation comfortable for you?
- Where in the body did you feel that it was comfortable?
- Did you share your experience with everyone? If yes, what was the response? If no, why not?
- What do you think made it feel comfortable?
- What would you do if you were in the situation again and someone else shared with you that they did not feel comfortable?

Self-awareness sharing circle (30 minutes)

Invite students to share their recalls in pairs and ask them to listen without speaking or asking questions. Allow ten minutes per person (five minutes per recall). After 20 minutes, ask students to share with each other how they felt sharing this and how they think they were perceived by the other person listening (two minutes each for sharing, two minutes for responding).

Insights and actions for further self-awareness development (30 minutes)

Ask students to identify two insights from the conversation and two actions that would enhance their self-awareness.

The above activities enhance students' self-awareness (understanding and perception of themselves), which in turn allows them to become more compassionate towards themselves and others. In particular, these techniques can improve conflict management and sense of belonging and wellbeing among students (Usprech & Lam, 2020).

7.3 Self-care and mindfulness for future leaders

Taking time to tap into our awareness in order to manage our selves and challenging situations better is a form of self-care. It requires appreciation of the self as an entity that can grow and develop (Dweck, 2009). Self-care starts by giving our selves permission to take time for ourselves. In my own experience of working with business students the permission piece is the hardest part because of the pressures students experience in the final year and their anticipation of working life. Those who want to pursue a demanding city job especially feel that there is little space and time for self-care and that this would not be perceived as welcome by respective companies. Students are often surprised to learn that research has shown leaders who are self-caring are more compassionate. Thus, leaders are more likely to also feel compassionate towards their employees and encourage employees to look after themselves by taking time for self-care (Klug et al., 2022). In fact, employees rated leaders who took time for self-care more highly and leader self-care has been found to be a determinant of healthy leadership.

Invite students to explore self-care as a topic and practice. Research in favour of self-care leaders and what it means can be an eye-opener for students and ensure that they consider self-care to be part of a work–life balance. An exercise that can be helpful is to brainstorm different self-care options and to draw up a self-care package. Here are some guiding questions for small group activities:

1. What do you think self-care is?
2. When is self-care important?
3. What self-care tools could you think of?
4. When do you think these tools are effective?
5. What are your thoughts about self-care promotion in the working environment?

Case study: Managing self-care at work

> Imagine you have just started your first job in a medium-sized company. It was not your first choice, but they offered you good benefits, and your line manager seems to be nice and supportive of bringing you on board. You are introduced to a colleague who has been at the company for six months. Your colleague is a similar age to you. You are assigned on a project together, which you are both enthusiastic about. Two weeks into the project, you notice that your colleague is tired and exhausted at work. Coming in late and leaving early are some of the behaviours. Sometimes you receive a text from your colleague that something came up. The last time you worked together, your colleague complained about a headache. You feel like you are on your own managing the project. Your line manager checks in regularly with both of you, but neither your colleague nor the line manager mention anything. You start to feel uncertain about what to do. The project is becoming more and more demanding, you notice that your worries have increased, and the situation is impacting your sleep. What are you going to do?

Case study questions:

1. How could you manage the situation at work?
2. What do you need to look after yourself?
3. What would you expect from your colleague?
4. If you were in the shoes of your colleague, how would you like your co-worker to react?
5. What would you do if you were the line manager?

   The situation has impacted your sleep how could you address that and ensure that you have a good night's sleep? Explore the following questions:

1. What do you know about the importance of sleep for wellbeing?
2. How important is sleep for you?
3. What is your sleep routine?
4. How has your sleep pattern changed since you started working?
5. What strategies could you use to get good sleep?

Invite students to share their answers and support them in developing a self-care approach that would help them to manage the situation based on scientific evidence.

7.4 Assessing students' mindfulness skills

Developing mindfulness skills, including self-awareness and knowing how to access internal resources in an effective and sustainable manner, requires commitment and an openness to change. The intention of this module is not to assess students' ability to facilitate mindfulness sessions but rather to finesse for a mindful approach towards themselves. The learning outcomes for the module reflect this intention, which we believe are transferable into any career path students might choose. We deliberately did not use the word mindful in the learning outcomes. Instead, awareness, sustainability, and resourcefulness which centre around mindfulness are the themes we refer to.

1. Demonstrate development of self-awareness in the context of managing their career effectively.
2. Critically evaluate different career paths and support insights with literature.
3. Reflect on their personal and professional development and identify a sustainable future career path.
4. Apply knowledge, skills, attitudes and behaviours acquired throughout the module to identify a career path that is resourceful and sustainable.

Students are assessed against the learning outcomes by means of two summative assessments of equal weight: a poster presentation and an individual reflective and prospective account.

Assessment 1: Post presentation

The poster presentation asks students to work in pairs and to interview two individuals about their career paths and how they manage their career. Individuals should have been in employment for a minimum of ten years. If the interviewees are family members, then students are encouraged to swap interviewer so that there is some emotional distance between interviewees and interviewers. Students must obtain participant consent for the interviews to be audio recorded and information to be used as part of their module evaluation. Interview procedure and conduct abide by university regulations for conducting research,, including GDPR, ethics, and consent forms. Students are not required to seek ethical approval to conduct interviews unless research insights are used for wider publication.

The posters should give a visual overview of milestones and coping strategies individuals had used to manage challenging situations or make decisions for better wellbeing and work–life balance. A set of open-ended questions to assist interviews is provided in advance. Below are ten questions that students can follow and use to probe further.

1. What does success mean to you?
2. Has your understanding of success changed over time?
3. What does self-awareness mean to you?
4. How self-aware were you at the beginning of your career?
5. How has your self-awareness changed over time?
6. How do you feel about self-care? How important do you believe it is that leaders are self-caring?
7. How would you describe your career path?
8. Are you happy to share any challenges you have experienced over the course of your career that have had an impact on your wellbeing or work–life balance?
9. How did you go about these challenges? What strategies or support did you use?
10. What are three tools that you put in your 'managing my career toolbox'?

The posters will be displayed in one of the seminar sessions, and students are asked to choose one poster that they believe has had a profound impact on their learning. They will take those insights into the second assessment as part of their reflection. The creation of the posters should help students to develop greater self-awareness and learn about how others have manged their careers, what resources they tapped into (internal and external), and how sustainable their careers were thereof.

Assessment 2: Reflective and prospective account

The reflective and prospective account gives students space to synthesise and evaluate their learning and adopt a new perspective towards managing their career in the future. We particularly want students to be aware of the availability and accessibility of their own internal resources and how to best use them for their mental, emotional, and physical benefit. The second assignment should highlight insights gained through the module and the take aways for the future including a list of their career self-management toolbox.

I have used reflection and prospection accounts as an assessment tool for many years. Students report that they enjoy the process of personal inquiry, some might even refer to it as introspection. Both reflection and prospection have qualities that develop, improve and cultivate a greater sense of self, self-knowledge, and self-awareness (Ardelt & Grunwald, 2018; Nesbit, 2007; Saunders et al., 2007). Most of us are probably far more familiar with reflection, the looking back into the past and learning from the past, understanding how our actions and decisions in the past impact our present moment experience. Reflection creates greater self-awareness and enables managers to regulate emotions and learn from insights gained through introspection (Nesbit, 2007). Throughout the book, some mediations and coaching questions are built on the construct of reflection. You can use these to support students to learn to become more reflective and reflexive.

Prospection is less well used in academic assessment approaches, and yet it is equally powerful. Prospection is a teleological construct (Bronk & Mitchell, 2022) which helps individuals to imagine different future scenarios for themselves and utilise those insights to positively affect their present moment experience including behaviours (Baumeister et al., 2016). It is not uncommon that prospection is built on an individual's expectation and desire of what the future holds (Oettingen & Mayer, 2002). I use prospection regularly as a tool in coaching and for meditation through visualisation. Perhaps it is helpful for students to practise prospection by means of meditation or creative mapping. At the end of this chapter, you will find a short meditation that uses prospection to identify purpose.

However, it is worth noting that anticipating possible positive futures for ourselves is not always the case (Bronk & Mitchell, 2022). Sometimes students hold negative beliefs about the future which prevents them entering a prospective space, which makes practice and understanding how to change belief patterns an important consideration for this type of assessment. The inability of students to prospect could be triggered by multiple rejections received as part of job hunting. If you experience a student struggling to prospect, have a conversation and perhaps refer the student to the wellbeing support or career services available in your institution. It can be helpful to narrow the time frame for prospection. I use a time window of a maximum of 12 months. In addition, a conversation around prospection might yield a discussion on purpose with students (Bronk & Mitchell, 2022). Being able to envisage a positive future instils a sense of purpose in students. The greater students' knowledge is about self-awareness, resourcefulness, and inner sustainability, the more easily they will be able to identify a purpose, which becomes a prospective construct.

Meditation (10 min) prospection of desire and purpose

> Find a comfortable seat, cross-legged on the floor or on a chair. Place your feet on the ground and your hands on your thighs palms facing up or down. Feel the connection between the sit bones and the chair or cushion. Feel the weight of your hands on your thighs. Become aware of your inhale and exhale.
>
> With your next inhale, lengthen through the spine, and as you exhale, drop the shoulders, feel the weight on the chair a little more. Let's do this one more time. Inhale lengthen; exhale, relax, loosen up, let go of tension in the body and in the mind. Centre your awareness on what you are feeling and experiencing right here, right now.
>
> This meditation uses visualisation and an ancient mantra. The mantra is borrowed from the classic Indian book, the Bhagavad Gita. In chapter 2 verse 48 Arjuna is advised by Krishna to establish himself in the present moment and then perform an action, which in Sanskrit is written as *yogastah kuru karmani*.

We will use this mantra, *yogastah kuru karmani*, after visualisation to recentre our awareness.

Take a couple of long slow breaths. Imagine you are graduating from university. It is a warm day. People are happy and celebrating. You are happy and celebrating. Imagine what that feels like. You have accomplished what you set out to do. Notice where in the body you experience a sense of accomplishment. Maybe there is a smile, butterflies, or a tingling. It is all good. Feel it. Bathe in it.

You are continuing with your celebration, and a friend asks you what your future plans are. You feel excited about the future, and you share that you have recently accepted a job offer that perfectly suits your skills, interests, and values. You are so looking forward to starting work, to getting to know the people in the company. You share that you attended an onboarding event a couple of days ago. Everybody was friendly. You sat down with your line manager, and you talked about potential projects and future career opportunities within the company. You felt supported with a sense of being able to grow. Your desire to work in an area that excites you and the opportunity to talk about the future have given you a feeling of purpose. You can see that the future is bright and that your future has great opportunities.

Take a moment, and cultivate that feeling of excitement and purpose. Smile to yourself, and establish yourself in the present moment before we take it deeper. [One minute of stillness and silence.]

Now set yourself an intention for how your career path starts and unfolds. Become really clear about success on the way and feelings of joy. Whatever you imagine, be bold, be brave, and be courageous, and then plant this intention in your heart space. Place your hands on your heart and take a long deep breath in. Now let the thoughts and feelings go. Bring your attention back to the breath, to the here and now.

We are going to use the mantra *yogastah kuru karmani* to allow our connection with our desires to deepen. We will speak the mantra for about two minutes. You can also whisper it or silently repeat it in your head. [Instructor speaks mantra out loud for two minutes.] After two minutes, we will remain in silence, and we will allow the stillness to settle in. Return to your intention in your heart and bathe in it. [After two minutes ring the chimes or use a gentle tone of voice to bring students back into the room.]

When you are ready take a long deep breath in, and let it go. Let's do this one more time. Take a long deep breath in, and release. Open your eyes, take in the room around you, and write down anything that has arisen for you, that has come up for you. [Give students five minutes to journal and perhaps add some time for sharing experiences.]

Chapter 7 in a nutshell...

Creating a mindfulness module for business programmes is not hard, but to design it in a way that it has purpose beyond knowledge acquisition and longer-term relevance is hard because it requires educators to position it under the umbrella of *What is in it for me?* We might not be comfortable with that, but intrinsic motivation is stronger than extrinsic motivation.

Intrinsic motivation can be activated if something is important to us, if we care about it, because we want to benefit from it. Three key aspects underpin the development of modules informed by mindfulness or with the goal of supporting students to become more mindful: relevance for the future, benefits for now, and assessment. Before hitting the drawing board ask:

1. How is mindfulness relevant to future leaders? What do graduates want? One answer might be, to secure a job, to be successful, to be confident. Use those insights and topics to scaffold learning aims and outcomes and content.
2. What are the benefits for students now to learn about the foundations of mindfulness? Perhaps it is about becoming more resilient and self-aware. Again, bring these insights into the development and design of the module structure and assessment.
3. What do you want to assess, skills, knowledge, application? What are students interested in learning about that they cannot retrieve from the internet, ChatGTP, or watch on YouTube? Use these anchors to devise an assessment strategy that aligns with relevance and benefits.

Invite curiosity into your classes not just critical thinking. I would like to close this chapter with the following questions from Verse 44, *Tao Te Ching*, 'True Freedom' (Tzu, 2021), which I sometimes use to kick start the mindfulness journey in class: '*Which is better fame or integrity? Why? Which is more valuable, riches or good character? Why? Which is more dangerous failure or success? Why?*'.

References

Amoroso, L. M., & Burke, M. (2018). Developing career-ready business students: Three curriculum models. *Journal of Education for Business*, 93(8), 420–429.

Ardelt, M., & Grunwald, S. (2018). The importance of self-reflection and awareness for human development in hard times. *Research in Human Development*, 15(3–4), 187–199.

Baumeister, R. F., Vohs, K. D., & Oettingen, G. (2016). Pragmatic prospection: How and why people think about the future. *Review of general psychology*, 20(1), 3–16.

Bronk, K. C., & Mitchell, C. (2022). Considering purpose through the lens of prospection. *The Journal of Positive Psychology*, 17(2), 281–287.

Diver, A., & Lock, D. A. (2019). Constructing careers: Self-awareness, self-reflection, and self-efficacy amongst undergraduate business students. In A. Diver (Ed.). *Employability via higher education: Sustainability as scholarship*, (pp. 373–388). Springer. https://doi.org/10.1007/978-3-030-26342-3_24.

Dries, N. (2011). The meaning of career success. *Career Development International*, 16(4), 364–384. https://doi.org/10.1108/13620431111158788.

Dweck, C. S. (2009). Mindsets: Developing talent through a growth mindset. *Olympic Coach*, 21(1), 4–7.

Gammie, B., Gammie, E., & Cargill, E. (2002). Personal skills development in the accounting curriculum. *Accounting Education*, 11(1), 63–78.

Goldstein, J. (2013). *Mindfulness: A practical guide to awakening*. Sounds True.
Goleman, D. (2011). Emotional mastery. *Leadership Excellence*, 28(6), 12–13.
Gowan, M. A. (2012). Employability, well-being and job satisfaction following a job loss. *Journal of Managerial Psychology*, 27(8), 780–798.
Jamison, D. (2010). Leadership and professional development: An integral part of the business curriculum. *Business Education Innovation Journal*, 2(2).
Jennings, N., Lovett, S., Cuba, L., Swingle, J., & Lindkvist, H. (2013). What would make this a successful year for you? How students define success in college. *Liberal Education*, 99(2), 40–47.
Klug, K., Felfe, J., & Krick, A. (2022). Does self-care make you a better leader? A multisource study linking leader self-care to health-oriented leadership, employee self-care, and health. *International Journal of Environmental Research and Public Health*, 19(11), 6733.
Lawrence, E., Dunn, M. W., & Weisfeld-Spolter, S. (2018). Developing leadership potential in graduate students with assessment, self-awareness, reflection and coaching. *Journal of Management Development*, 37(8), 634–651.
Nesbit, P. (2007, December 4–11). *Self-awareness, self-reflection and self-regulation: an integrated model of managerial self-development* [Conference presentation]. Australian and New Zealand Academy of Management Conference, Sydney, Australia.
Oettingen, G., & Mayer, D. (2002). The motivating function of thinking about the future: expectations versus fantasies. *Journal of personality and social psychology*, 83(5), 1198.
Omar, A., Miah, M., & Nkabyo, E. (2015). Curriculum and Professional Development. *International Journal of Advanced and Innovative Research*, 4(3). 291–297.
Page, M. L. (2016). *The elusive meaning of success for student and tutors in a business school: A learning and teaching project*. https://core.ac.uk/download/pdf/323895166.pdf.
Rivers, C., & O'Brien, J. (2019). Developing business-ready graduates: Teaching inside out. In H. T. Bui, H. T. Nguyen, and D. Cole (Eds.), *Innovate higher education to enhance graduate employability* (pp. 83–94). Routledge.
Rubens, A., Schoenfeld, G. A., Schaffer, B. S., & Leah, J. S. (2018). Self-awareness and leadership: Developing an individual strategic professional development plan in an MBA leadership course. *The International Journal of Management Education*, 16(1), 1–13.
Sauer, S., & Kohls, N. (2011). Mindfulness in leadership: Does being mindful enhance leaders' business success? In: S. Han, & E. Pöppel (Eds.), *Culture and neural frames of cognition and communication. On thinking*. (pp. 287–307). Springer. https://doi.org/10.1007/978-3-642-15423-2_17.
Saunders, P. A., Tractenberg, R. E., Chaterji, R., Amri, H., Harazduk, N., Gordon, J. S., Lumpkin, M., & Haramati, A. (2007). Promoting self-awareness and reflection through an experiential mind-body skills course for first year medical students. *Medical teacher*, 29(8), 778–784.
Spronken-Smith, R., & Walker, R. (2010). Can inquiry-based learning strengthen the links between teaching and disciplinary research? *Studies in Higher Education*, 35(6), 723–740.
Tzu, L. (2021). *Tao Te Ching. The book of the way*. Ancient Renewal.
Usprech, J., & Lam, G. (2020, June 18 – 21). Self-awareness and empathy as tools to mitigate conflict, promote wellness, and enhance performance in a third-year engineering design course. *Proceedings of the Canadian Engineering Education Association (CEEA)*. https://doi.org/10.24908/pceea.vi0.14163.

8
MINDFULNESS COACHING AND BUSINESS EDUCATION

Throughout the previous chapters, coaching questions played an integral part in merging mindfulness and business education. Coaching questions are a great way to create space and agency for management students and academics and an opportunity for them to reflect on their state of being, to become more self-aware and present and develop capabilities to manage and lead more effectively in the future.

I started my coaching journey in 2017 and decided to train as an executive coach with the Association of Executive Coaching in London. The business school funded my training as part of my professional development, and I have since coached hundreds of students and colleagues within and outside my institution. In the beginning, I focused on supporting students and colleagues to improve academic performance and build confidence. Many frameworks and coaching models were helpful along the way (Carey et al., 2011; Libri, 2004; Panchal & Riddell, 2020) until I found my own method of coaching. I noticed that building confidence was far more important to students and academic peers than improving performance; in fact, performance improved because confidence increased (Compte & Postlewaite, 2004; Hollenbeck & Hall, 2004). Low confidence led to anxiety, self-doubt (Verducci, 2014), regurgitation of old beliefs, and an inability to relax and let go. Because I have suffered from the same symptoms and found mindfulness and particularly meditation helpful, I decided to introduce meditation as a tool to my students and colleagues. In the session, we explore anxiety, self-doubt, and old beliefs in the context of their work or studies and build confidence. The feedback was so positive that I continued to integrate other mindfulness tools such as yoga and breath work. Clients reported that these strategies were far more effective than talking for an hour. The tools helped them to develop a sense of appreciation and gratitude for themselves for what they have

DOI: 10.4324/9781032637464-12

achieved, which increased their confidence to manage and lead inside and outside the classroom. Mindfulness coaching became my way of working with students and colleagues in partnership.

In this chapter, I share the benefits and principles of mindfulness coaching in business school contexts: mindfulness coaching for personal tutors, peer to peer mindfulness coaching to develop self-awareness, and mindfulness coaching for educators to enhance their own learning and teaching.

8.1 Coaching in business education

Coaching as an approach for developing leaders and learning model in business education has been discussed in the literature for a while (Eriksen et al., 2020; Reid et al., 2020; Yanovska et al., 2019). Most studies identify coaching as a valuable tool to support student personal and professional development. Coaching used effectively has a motivating effect on individuals (Goleman, 2011) because the premise of coaching is to empower the coachee through questions and active listening (Bakhshandeh, 2023; Weger Jr et al., 2014) in such a way that answers emerge through the coachees' own investigation (Celoria & Hemphill, 2014). The person takes centre stage. This is also referred to as person-oriented approach (Lemisiou, 2018).

In business education, coaching is mostly introduced as part of leadership modules or courses, either stand-alone or as part of professional development streams in master's or MBA programmes (Eriksen et al., 2020; Thomason et al., 2022). Courses consist of knowledge acquisition and peer coaching. The latter is an experiential learning method that students find challenging if following the principles of coaching: no judgment, active listening, asking open questions, and being comfortable with silence instead of interrupting, offering advice and opinions, and mentoring the other person. Developing those skills takes time and careful planning from facilitators and it is recommended that coaching introduced as a learning and teaching model in business education is carried out by those who are trained as coaches through a certified and accredited coach training organisation or who actively work as coaches. Coaching has been accepted as a useful and effective skill for developing leadership qualities and competencies (Liu et al., 2021). However, focus has been predominantly on improving performance and professional growth of individuals with high potential in the future (Gan et al., 2021) and less so on how to use coaching to support individuals, in the moment, to address challenges and explore emotions, thought patterns, and beliefs that might hold them back. People who struggle at work or face challenges, regardless of their potential, are less likely to be offered coaching opportunities. They are more likely to be referred to occupational health or wellbeing centres, yet there is an opportunity to utilise coaching in a way that supports individuals with different needs.

118 Mindfulness and Business Education

In my experience and work with students and staff, coaching can have profound benefits for their wellbeing and in turn improve performance, which can move them from not being perceived as high achieving or someone with a potential for higher responsibility roles to someone who is very capable. However, I found that traditional coaching models (e.g. solution-focused coaching, GROW model) and approaches are less useful to support development of students and staff who are not already achieving highly, whereas mindfulness coaching builds upon person-centred coaching approaches.

8.2 Mindfulness coaching

The marriage of mindfulness and coaching is not surprising given the demanding and noisy world of work most of us live in, and students are not exempt. Students experience even higher levels of stress and pressure to succeed in their studies, market themselves differently, and distinguish themselves from the competition in a way that makes them stand out. Thus, mindfulness coaching sessions for students often centre around the questions of: Who am I? How am I different and unique? Questions that bring us back to the concepts of self-awareness, self-confidence, knowing and acting in a certain way. Despite the demand for students to find answers to these questions, mindfulness coaching is not established as a common practice in business schools yet.

One reason is that business academics who are trained and certified as coaches are few and far between. In contrast, it is more likely that practitioners transitioning into business education are qualified executive coaches. Another reason is that there are even fewer academics, as established earlier in the book, who are qualified or interested in facilitating mindfulness sessions or introducing mindfulness-based techniques. At present there simply is no research and empirical evidence on mindfulness coaching in business education that would demonstrate its effectiveness. However, there is limited research that confirms the benefits of mindfulness-based coaching processes on wellbeing and performance in the workplace (Shelly & Zaidman, 2023), education (Corti & Gelati, 2020), and other industries (Van Den Assem & Passmore, 2022; Shelly & Zaidman, 2023). Shelly and Zaidman's study is unique in its conduct, and findings indicate significant changes and benefits to participants who engaged in the mindfulness-based coaching sessions. The benefits include growth in self-awareness, the ability to engage with multiple perspectives, and effective stress management. In addition, researchers identified an increase in compassion, kindness, and friendliness. Participants engaged in weekly coaching sessions over a period of 12 weeks and kept journals. Interviews were conducted after completion of the coaching sessions and two years after the study took place. Participants reported benefits of mindfulness-based coaching (Satya method), even after two years, and a positive impact beyond their working environment. These findings confirm my own experiences and those shared by my students and colleagues. Being part of someone's transformational journal is very rewarding, especially if the benefits are far greater than we can imagine. I believe that this is part of our responsibility as business educators to support and equip students with the skills to access their internal resources.

I feel privileged to have had the opportunity to qualify as both a coach and a mindfulness practitioner through separate teacher training paths: yoga teacher, meditation teacher, and breath work instructor. Training with different organisations has helped me to sharpen my tools, go deeper into each of them and learn from others. In addition, I was able to practise and research the impact of each tool on student learning and staff development over the years and slowly build mindfulness coaching into my learning and teaching philosophy and approach. However, the toolbox is endless I continue to add to it as I go along. Someone once told me *once you open the box of mindfulness you never close it, and it keeps on giving*.

Alongside meditation, breath work, and yoga, I also use journaling, coaching cards, and creative mapping or art-based approaches to support sessions. It is worthwhile mentioning that mindfulness coaching is governed by the same principles as conventional coaching including listening, questioning, clarifying, and reflecting (Thomas & Smith, 2005). The only difference is that mindfulness coaching is concerned with establishing oneself in the present moment, bringing awareness to what is happening right here right now, not just by asking questions but through guided meditation, movement, breathing exercises. It is about the alignment of body and mind and often about quieting the mind in a way that allows the coaches to gather insights that can be useful in developing better study or management and leadership skills. Insight might be around reframing situations, identifying values, passions, aspirations, strengths and weaknesses, and the impact we want to have on ourselves and others. The foundations of mindfulness guide the questions throughout the coaching process. Observation of thoughts, emotions, language, and behaviours in a non-judgemental way enables coachees to access their awareness.

Mindfulness coaching starts with setting an intention, formulated by the coachee. This could relate to an immediate or short-term phenomenon or goal usually set within the next couple of weeks. The intention can become the focus of the session, but sometimes it shifts throughout the session as coach and coachee uncover its layers. At the end of the coaching session, the coachee formulates actions. For this purpose, I use the SMART framework, which gives coachees a tangible way of knowing, applying, and measuring. SMART refers to S – specific, M – measurable, A – action oriented, R – realistic, and T – timely. We review the SMART at the beginning of the next session and set a new intention. The mindfulness tools (e.g. specific meditations, breathing exercises) introduced to coachees throughout the session often become part of one's SMART, which in turn supports students and academics to develop their own mindfulness practice and change behaviour in the long term.

8.3 Mindfulness coaching for business students

Mindfulness coaching and personal tutoring

The most likely scenario in which business educators would apply mindfulness coaching tools is in their capacity as personal tutors. The role of a personal tutor is to provide pastoral care to students around academic and sometimes personal aspects. When I started out as a personal tutor, I admit that it felt a bit forced to meet with students two or three times a semester and ask about how they were doing. I was inexperienced and less confident in building trust and a meaningful student tutor relationship, let alone thinking about creating a safe space. I simply was not aware of the importance of it, which most early career academics who I onboard concur with. A typical personal tutor session would unfold like this:

TUTOR: *Hello, come in. Have a seat. Good to see you. How are you? How are your studies going?*
STUDENT: *Thanks. I am fine. All going well.*
TUTOR: *Mmm. Great. Do you have any favourite classes? Things you enjoy?*
STUDENT: *Yeah. I like the marketing seminars.*
TUTOR: *Great. Any other classes you like or dislike?*
STUDENT: *I don't like the finance classes. I'm not good at maths.*
TUTOR: *Oh, I completely understand. I didn't like them either. I was always worried and anxious about the exams. Okay, well, is there anything else I can help you with? Anything you would like to ask?*
STUDENT: *Mmm. No. Well, do you know how I can get my library card replaced?*

Personal tutor sessions would be unplanned, unfocused, and uneventful. So much so that personal tutor hours are not utilised as a resource by students, which is not surprising given the above. Since I learned to train as a coach, I applied my knowledge to these sessions, and my relationship with my students has changed. However, I also developed a framework for personal tutors to guide their sessions that is based around the idea of coaching, called SEEC – supporting, empowering, enhancing, connecting.

Supporting refers to identifying resources that can help students throughout their study journey. This could be regulations, code of conducts, handbooks, etc. Empowering is concerned with any aspects of university life that a student needs help with, from work-based experiences to goal setting, wellbeing, and interpersonal skills development. Enhancing encompasses all aspects of academic development including progression or choosing optional modules. Connecting enables students to access societies, events, and networks offered by the university and any services for employability and careers management.

The framework became a useful tool to assess the needs of students and add value to a personal tutor session. Yet, the SEEC model did not help me to change the nature of the meeting initially. I asked myself what my intention for personal tutor meetings was and how I could tune into the students' emotional world so I could provide the pastoral care they needed? My intention has been to build a relationship with students in a way that supports their academic needs whether they were in distress or not. I liked the idea of tuning in and used it to frame my personal tutor meetings. TUNE stands for *Trust – Us – Needs – Evaluate*.

Any relationship is built on trust, and it requires at least two people. In this case the student and the tutor, which I call *us*. Based on my intention and the value I want to provide, knowing and understanding my student's needs is paramount to support them appropriately. However, I also need to be able to evaluate which support is the best for the student and whether my support was effective. The following scenario between myself and Max a first year undergraduate business management student demonstrates the application of TUNE:

TUTOR: *Welcome, Max. Have a seat; make yourself comfortable. Take your time. It looks like you've hurried to come to the meeting. Just take your time and breathe.*

[I give students a little bit of time to settle in and breathe as they often arrive holding their breath.]

MAX: *Yes, I've come straight from the lecture, I didn't want to be late.*
TUTOR: *No problem. You are here now. How was the lecture?*

[A short exchange takes place about the experience of the lecture, and if it is the first session, I will introduce myself, share a little bit about myself, and invite the student to share something too.]

TUTOR: *What are your hobbies?*
MAX: *I play football, I hope to get into the university team, but it seems competitive. Not sure; the trials are later today.*
TUTOR: *Football is a great sport. Have you played for a team before?*
MAX: *Yes, I played for X and the school team. I love it, so I don't want to give it up.*
TUTOR: *That's wonderful. Most students enjoy playing sports on Wednesday afternoon. We might have to find a different day for our meetings in the future because most games are when our tutor session is. Don't worry we'll work it out. How are your studies going at the moment? What do you enjoy, and is there anything you are worried about?*
MAX: *It's going well. I like most subjects. I'm a little bit worried about financial accounting. I'm not good at maths. I think I understand it all when I'm in the lecture and seminar, but then I go home, and I can't remember anything, and I struggle with the homework.*
TUTOR: *It's great that you revise and give the homework a go. What do you think would help you?*

MAX: *Not sure; I am just not good at maths. Never was. I feel anxious about it, and I avoid it, so I sometimes just don't do the homework or don't complete it.*
TUTOR: *Are you doing your homework alone? Would you be able to work with someone maybe?*
MAX: *Maybe. My mate is good at it.*
TUTOR: *How do you feel about asking him to help you?*
MAX: *Yeah, could do. I just wish I didn't feel so apprehensive.*
TUTOR: *Tell me more about that feeling? …*

It takes a while to build trust and create a safe environment and relationship with a student. Unlike other professions, we usually have time to connect with students and go deeper. I appreciate that exploring feelings with students might not be something that some academics are partial to or find easy. Learning the principles of mindfulness coaching as part of our role as personal tutors would have a significant positive impact on student lives. Once, the connection is made, students open up and appreciate the time we take to help them connect to themselves. Of course, if they want to explore it more deeply, we can refer them to wellbeing and psychological services, but sometimes all it takes is to give them the space to articulate their feelings around fear and worry. I agreed with the above student to meet him a couple more times before the exam, and we did some breathing exercises, which he also used before revising. He learned to prepare his body and mind in a similar way to warming up before a football match. This analogy was helpful for him, and he passed the exam successfully. In addition, we used affirmations to change his old beliefs about not being good at maths. The first step was to break the homework into chunks instead of seeing it as a big threat. He noticed that he was capable of reading the instructions and identifying the steps. He used affirmations such as:

I understand the task.
I take it one step at a time.
I take my time to focus on collecting all the information.
I am okay with taking my time.
I write down questions that arise.
It is okay to ask for help from my tutor.

These affirmation sound simple and yet they are very powerful because they give the student permission to slow down, to seek help, and to learn that this is okay, that there is nothing wrong. By the end of the first semester, Max became more self-aware, confident, and kind with himself. Seraj and Leggett (2023) highlight that coaching as part of personal tutoring increases student motivation, independence, and confidence, and participants in their study agreed that a coaching approach would enhance tutor and tutee relationships. The latter is important because we are usually assigned personal tutees for the duration of their studies, which in some cases can be years.

Peer to peer mindfulness coaching

Most business schools have a strong focus on employability and offer workshops that focus on developing skills relevant to and necessary for entering the world of work. These workshops are usually skill-based and are either, as explained in previous chapters, embedded in an employability stream and part of the curriculum or offered as extracurricular. In addition, some business schools offer their students one-to-one coaching opportunities to explore aspects of employability. I worked with several postgraduate students over the years, and I was privileged to be part of some transformational and successful journeys. Of course, scalability is limited with one-to-one coaching but peer-to-peer coaching offers the opportunity to not just reach more students at once but to support students in developing mindfulness coaching skills themselves. The most challenging aspect for students is learning to listen and to not interject with questions (Eriksen et al., 2020).

We integrated peer-to-peer mindfulness coaching as part of a one-day employability workshop that focused on developing self-awareness. The workshop was split into two parts. The morning session focuses on internal self-awareness and the afternoon session on external self-awareness (Eurich, 2018). The workshop starts by exploring what self-awareness is and we use a range of open-ended questions to engage students in the conversation. Open-ended questions are targeted at internal self-awareness and relevant to each student. Below is a list of questions that we use to guide students in their exploration.

Developing internal self-awareness questions

- How self-aware do you think you are on a scale of 1 to 5 (5 is very self-aware, 1 not so self-aware)? Give reasons for your choice.
- What is self-awareness?
- Why do you need to be self-aware?
- Why do you want to master it?
- What types of self-awareness can you think of?

The discussion of these questions might take place as an open forum, a sharing circle, or perhaps it is nicer for students to discuss in pairs or small groups. It depends on the nature of the group, and I keep an open mind about how to facilitate the discursive exploration. At this point in the workshop students are not aware of the distinction between internal and external self-awareness. I tend to bring this differentiation into the conversation at the end of the morning, once we have established a sense of self-awareness on a broader scale. In the beginning, students might share that self-awareness is about feedback, experiences, learning and impact. Unpacking each of them takes time, and students often use stories to explain their thinking. The learning aspect is most strongly developed in our understanding of self-awareness. Students refer to developing skills about how to handle situations, regulate emotions, learn to respond differently. Self-awareness has a relational quality to ourselves and others, and it is a meta skill that we humans are eager to master. Why do we want to master it? At this point students start to become more analytical and explore self-awareness from different perspectives of learning, knowledge about self, and knowledge about others with the goal of knowing strengths and weaknesses, preferences, likes, and triggers. Interestingly students feel that knowing oneself is helpful with not wasting time. At the same time, they acknowledge that learned and experienced knowledge are two different approaches in the quest of mastering self-awareness and that the acquisition is a journey, a process with room for mistakes. After the conversation, students gain insights about how thoughts, emotions, sensations contribute to the way we develop self-awareness and perceive ourselves. That the body is instrumental in the process as a tool for communicating how we perceive ourselves, how we perceive others, and how we are perceived by others. The conversations are rich and invite a deep dive into our internal world. The following questions are used to guide that process:

- What are your values? What are your passions? What are your aspirations?
- What physical clues do you notice that allow you to become aware of yourself?
- What emotional clues do you notice that allow you to become aware of yourself?
- What thoughts do you notice that allow you to become aware of yourself?

Mindfulness and self-awareness exercises

The answers to these questions are not immediately discussed. Students use their answers to scaffold and frame their peer-to-peer coaching activity in the afternoon. The time after individual reflection on deeper material provides good soil for mindfulness exercises. Meditation and breath work exercises are well suited to continuing the exploration. I call it attending to and tuning into self-awareness. The meditation starts with a short warm-up, followed by centring of awareness before I invite students to join a breath work exercise, to redirect attention to physical sensations, away from the mind, which was used heavily before. A lengthening inhale and exhale exercise with counting works well. For instance, inhale for the count of four, exhale for the count of four, inhale for the count of five, exhale for five, and so on until eight or ten. After breathing exercises, students are guided into relaxation using a body scan. Once the body is fully relaxed, I ask students some questions to return to their thoughts and prepare them for reflection time. Allocating 15 minutes after meditation for journaling and reflection is advised so that students can consolidate insights. Some might want to go for a walk or venture out into breakout spaces before a lunch break.

Mindfulness coaching tools

The afternoon introduces students to the model of mindfulness coaching to develop self-awareness through a short in person real time coaching demonstration. After the demo students are introduced to the basic skills required for facilitating peer-to-peer coaching. Thomas and Smith (2005) outline four basic skills of coaching, which we have adopted for the peer-to-peer coaching activity: questioning, listening, clarifying, reflecting.

Questioning

The art of asking questions is fundamental to facilitating coaching. We encourage students to use open-ended questions, which we have modelled throughout the day. Open-ended questions imply curiosity and leave room for coachees to expand and go deeper. These include what, when, where, how, why, and who. However, there are times when closed leading questions are helpful too.

Listening

Listening is the most difficult part of coaching for students (Seraj & Leggett, 2023). Demonstration is helpful for students to be aware that listening is just listening to the other person in silence with no response, either verbal or nonverbal. It is about holding space and creating space and time to think and elaborate while observing the coachee's body language and intuitively tuning into the patterns, tone, and what has perhaps not been said, while at the same time becoming aware of self-talk or questions that arise for the coach too. Making notes at times can support the student coach in this process.

Clarifying

Once one or more questions are answered, the student coach can ask for clarification to help the student coachee to dive deeper. Clarification might include follow-up, confirming and challenger questions in regard to statements.

Reflecting

After the peer coaching activity students are asked to reflect on the process based on four questions related to developing internal and external self-awareness. The first two questions relate to internal self-awareness, questions three and four refer to external self-awareness.

1. How did you perceive yourself?
2. How did you perceive the other person/ coach?
3. How do you think you were perceived?
4. How would you like to have been perceived?

During the peer-to-peer coaching activity students are invited to incorporate mindfulness tools such as guiding through a simple breath work exercise or body scan. For this purpose, scripts are provided to support them. While students participated and experienced meditation and breathing exercises in the morning, facilitating short, guided mindfulness exercises themselves can be unfamiliar, so it is important to give them the option of practising it. In conversations, students shared that facilitating mindfulness exercises as part of the coaching helped them to understand the value of mindfulness tools beyond their own experience. They became curious about how it makes the other person feel and an increase in empathy and compassion was expressed.

Peer-to-peer mindfulness coaching, whether for developing self-awareness or something else is a powerful tool to support students become more present, compassionate, and confident, qualities that are key for future leaders, and as research has shown, that have long-lasting positive effects after the event (Corti & Gelati, 2020; Gan et al., 2021; Lemisiou, 2018).

8.4 Mindfulness coaching for business educators

In the same way as mindfulness coaching experience is transformational for students, mindfulness coaching has also been found to be influential and impactful for supporting business school academics in developing learning and teaching skills. As mentioned in the previous chapters, the integration of mindfulness and business education requires all stakeholders to be equipped with the skills, knowledge, and tools to make change happen. If we want future leaders to be more mindful in their decision making, then we need to find a way to build this ethos into our teaching. I will discuss this in more depth in Chapter 9: 'How to Build a Mindfulness-Based Business Education Strategy.'

When I completed my learning and teaching qualification in 2012, I felt I had a good theoretical understanding of different educational approaches but very little opportunity to reflect upon my own development, philosophy, and identity as an academic and educator. I was not equipped with the tools of reflection in a way that would enable me to question how I taught. Instead, I would read about ideas and concepts and embed them in the classroom with the hope that students would like it. I published a couple of papers about classroom experiences and developed a framework. However, reflection remained superficial, and I was not clear where I was heading nor who I was. My eagerness to learn and openness to innovation in the classroom and outside and passion for advancing business education to improve student experience was soon picked up by others. I was appointed as Director for Undergraduate Studies, then Postgraduate and MBA Studies, before being offered the role of Director for Learning and Teaching in the business school, which is equivalent to associate dean for education in other schools. I was thrown in at the deep end with knowledge and some skills and capabilities, mostly self-taught, but I would say little self-awareness in comparison to now. My comfort zone was non-existent, and I felt like a fraud and inadequate when I was offered the opportunity for coaching, but it was a game changer. Soon, I realised the benefits of coaching as a leader, educator, and person. The person-centric approach helped me to learn about myself and develop a different kind of self-awareness that was relevant to doing the work I was doing. The benefits were so great that I decided to embed coaching and reflection as core elements in a programme I developed for practitioners to transition into business school teaching: Postgraduate Certificate in Business and Management Education (Teacher Training) (PGCert). For this purpose, I embarked upon obtaining my own coaching qualification.

I started to coach colleagues in academia in 2018 within the programme and outside the programme. I have probably coached over one hundred academics internationally and gained great insights into how coaching can transform not just our own understanding of learning and teaching but the experience of students. At the time, coaching sessions were based on classical models (e.g. solution-focused, GROW, etc.). However, I soon realised that clients turned up stressed, not present, and with a need to slow down. Mindfulness offered an avenue and space for coachees to centre, to arrive in the space and give themselves permission to let go of the day so far. These short interventions signalled a welcome break to my clients and colleagues, and it was often this short period of time they wanted to experience and come back for. The integration of mindfulness techniques and wisdom into coaching has helped me to connect with clients and colleagues differently. Together we used mindfulness coaching to develop learning and teaching approaches and new ways of connecting with students (Reid et al., 2020).

Each coachee is different and has their own set of questions, aspirations, and dilemmas. Mindfulness coaching has enabled them to look inside and beyond themselves for inspiration. Some were so passionate that they wanted to share what they had tried out and how it impacted their students and themselves. I would like to share two success stories here. The first one is about a practitioner who joined the earlier cohorts of the PGCert. The second story is about an early career educator who joined the PGCert more recently. Both transformations are remarkable.

Charley worked in marketing for many years, and she kindly gave guest lectures for one of the marketing modules I led at the time. She has an open, approachable, and friendly demeanour and shared that her passion was for learning and working with young adults. Her sister passed away a couple of months before I met her, and she shared that she wanted to do something different with her life rather than continue in her high-stress job, become ill, and die like her sister. She joined the PGCert, and I became her personal learning coach. During the six months of the PGCert, Charley was juggling a full-time job and a young family. Finding a time and space where she could focus was challenging at times. She read a lot and was eager to share her knowledge. We mainly met online, which meant that she was in her home surrounded by situations that would require her attention. Her breathing was shallow, and she avoided going deeper into some of her explorations. While I understood her circumstances, I directed her attention to how I perceived her behaviour and how students would perceive it too. This was like an 'aha' moment for her. She did not expect to receive such feedback from me. I introduced her to breath work exercises and short meditations to settle in and encouraged her to keep a journal about how she perceived herself. After three months of weekly coaching our sessions were deep, and she dedicated time and space to her self-development. All the tools I shared with her including the foundations of mindfulness and concepts of embodied learning and teaching have shaped who she is today. She successfully transitioned into business school teaching and has not looked back since. She has recently received the teacher of the year award from her dean, and in her short speech, she referred to our sessions and the tools she now shares with her students.

Alex joined the PGCert as an early career academic in January 2024. Originally from the Middle East, Alex spent three years in industry and completing doctoral studies alongside that before securing a lecturing position at a business school in China. I could feel the passion for learning and teaching when we first met. Alex was open, happy to share, and not afraid to be vulnerable in the process, the opposite to Charley. Keeping track of Alex's ideas was challenging at times, and I suggested pausing for a moment to ask about it. Alex shared that this has always been a problem, too many ideas swirling round her head, and unfortunately this also happened in class, which meant that students would feel confused and unsure about what was relevant and what was not. Through meditation, Alex learned how to organise and label thoughts and how to use the breath to slow down thinking and speaking in class. In addition, we practised the skills of using coaching questions in the classroom instead of instantly providing a solution to a student query or problem. Alex became more mindful and patient with students, colleagues, and self. Every time we meet, Alex shares the benefits of these tools and how students are touched and responsive, how creating space for thinking has enabled her and the students to go deeper and there is no need to fill every second with information. In fact, Alex has become very skilled in holding space for silence and reflection with students and starts class with a short meditation. Teaching evaluations have improved significantly, and one of the students wrote to Alex after the exam:

You are the best lecturer I have had so far. I was really stressed about the exam, and then I remembered, you showed us how to close our eyes and focus on the breath. I did that, and I was able to finish the exam, I felt calmer. Thank you.

Zhuang Xie, undergraduate student, 2024

Chapter 8 in a nutshell...

Mindfulness coaching is a powerful tool to support students and academics on their journey to self-awareness and self-actualisation and it is applicable in many contexts of business education from personal tutoring to in class peer-to-peer group interactions and for academic self-development.

While writing this chapter, I received an email from our Centre for Wellbeing asking me to run more regular mindfulness coaching group sessions for students across the university. We are all in need of understanding the benefits of continuous self-development, and we, as educators, can act as a seed or as gardeners of the future by planting the seeds of what it means to lead kindly, and compassionately through self-awareness in the pursuit of living and leading a mindful community and life. I would like to close this chapter with Verse 17, 'Invisible Leader,' from *Tao Te Ching* (Tzu, 2021):

> *If a ruler lacks faith, so will the people. Unworthy rulers are despised. Common rulers are feared by their subjects. Good rulers win the affection and praise of their subjects. But when great rulers lead, they are hardly aware of their existence. How carefully wise rulers choose their words; how simple are their actions. Under such government, the people think they are ruling themselves.*

References

Bakhshandeh, B. (2023). Role of effective communication and active listening in building a coaching culture. In B. Bakhshandeh, & W. J. Rothwell (Eds.), *Building an organizational coaching culture: Creating effective environments for growth and success in organizations* (pp. 225–241). Routledge.

Carey, W., Philippon, D. J., & Cummings, G. G. (2011). Coaching models for leadership development: An integrative review. *Journal of leadership studies*, 5(1), 51–69.

Celoria, D., & Hemphill, D. (2014). Coaching from the coaches' perspective: a process-oriented focus. *International Journal of Mentoring and Coaching in Education*, 3(1), 72–85.

Compte, O., & Postlewaite, A. (2004). Confidence-enhanced performance. *American Economic Review*, 94(5), 1536–1557.

Corti, L., & Gelati, C. (2020). Mindfulness and coaching to improve learning abilities in university students: A pilot study. *International Journal of Environmental Research and Public Health*, 17(6), 1935.

Eriksen, M., Collins, S., Finocchio, B., & Oakley, J. (2020). Developing students' coaching ability through peer coaching. *Journal of Management Education*, 44(1), 9–38.

Eurich, T. (2018). What self-awareness really is (and how to cultivate it). *Harvard Business Review*, 4, 2–8.

Gan, G. C., Chong, C. W., Yuen, Y. Y., Yen Teoh, W. M., & Rahman, M. S. (2021). Executive coaching effectiveness: Towards sustainable business excellence. *Total Quality Management & Business Excellence*, 32(13–14), 1405–1423.

Goleman, D. (2011). Emotional mastery. *Leadership Excellence*, 28(6), 12–13.

Hollenbeck, G. P., & Hall, D. T. (2004). Self-confidence and leader performance. *Organizational dynamics*, 33(3), 254–269.

Lemisiou, M. A. (2018). The effectiveness of person-centered coaching intervention in raising emotional and social intelligence competencies in the workplace. *International Coaching Psychology Review*, 13(2), 6–26.

Libri, V. (2004). Beyond GROW: In search of acronyms and coaching models. *The International Journal of Mentoring and Coaching*, 2(1), 1–8.

Liu, Z., Venkatesh, S., Murphy, S. E., & Riggio, R. E. (2021). Leader development across the lifespan: A dynamic experiences-grounded approach. *The Leadership Quarterly*, 32(5), 101382.

Panchal, S., & Riddell, P. (2020). The GROWS model: extending the GROW coaching model to support behavioural change. *The Coaching Psychologist*, 16(2), 12–25.

Reid, A., Cook, J., Viedge, C., & Scheepers, C. B. (2020). Developing management effectiveness: The nexus between teaching and coaching. *The International Journal of Management Education*, 18(1), 100334.

Seraj, S., & Leggett, R. (2023). The challenges of personal tutoring in higher education: Applying a coaching approach at a UK higher education institution. *International Journal of Evidence Based Coaching & Mentoring*, 21(1).

Shelly, R., & Zaidman, N. (2023). Outcomes of mindfulness-based coaching for managers. *Coaching: An International Journal of Theory, Research and Practice*, 16(1), 31–48.

Thomas, W., & Smith, A. (2005). *Coaching solutions: Practical ways to improve performance in education*. Hawker Brownlow Education.

Thomason, S. J., Andersen, K., Gupta, P., & Rustogi, H. (2022). Enhancing experiential education in an MBA coaching program. *Journal of Education for Business*, 97(3), 196–203.

Tzu, L. (2021). *Tao Te Ching. The book of the way*. Ancient Renewal.

Van Den Assem, B., & Passmore, J. (2022). How experienced coaches use mindfulness in practice and how they know it is useful or beneficial. *Consulting Psychology Journal*, 74(1), 116–141. https://doi.org/10.1037/cpb0000219.

Verducci, S. (2014). Self-doubt: One moral of the story. *Studies in Philosophy and Education*, 33, 609–620.

Weger Jr, H., Castle Bell, G., Minei, E. M., & Robinson, M. C. (2014). The relative effectiveness of active listening in initial interactions. *International Journal of Listening*, 28(1), 13–31.

Yanovska, V., Baldzhy, M., & Fayvishenko, D. (2019). Coaching as a leadership style and a business education model. *Advances in Social Science, Education and Humanities Research*, 318, 210–214.

9
MINDFULNESS-DRIVEN BUSINESS EDUCATION STRATEGY

9.1 Strategy means choice

In 2005, Professor Peter Lorange (Lorange, 2005) of IMD Business School in Switzerland published an article in *Journal of Management Development* called 'Strategy Means Choice: Also for Today's Business School!' In the opening section Professor Lorange emphasised that human capital is essential in value-creation for organisations, and business schools need to think about how they are going to serve a new, knowledge-driven, networked society. He proclaimed an eclectic educational approach that includes action learning, web-based learning, role play and simulations. Moreover, students are likely to define the curriculum and demand a holistic learning environment, but more importantly, he predicted that students would become participants in the creation of learning, and that being the case, business schools must incorporate co-creation into their education strategy. The importance of business schools is to 'create' more than good practitioners (who they are, what they do, why, and how they do things). A business school's responsibility resides in developing inquisitive and curious minds that can 'reflect critically on their own, others' and societies' practice' (Clegg et al., 2013, p. 1258). The responsibility business schools hold to positively contribute to society has been voiced loud and clear by management scholars and, unsurprisingly, questions the ongoing role of business schools in developing globally responsible future leaders (Blass & Hayward, 2015). Education at the service of the person, instilling and cultivating the seed of leadership, and defining leadership as a virtue grounded in the idea that it can be learned and governed by prudence, temperance, fortitude, and justice are further recommendations made by management scholars (Osiemo, 2012). Such change requires a collective, multidisciplinary approach, a unified movement led by business schools and supported by youth work, industries, and other faculties within higher education (Blass & Hayward, 2015). But the question is how do we devise a business education strategy that does not just emphasise global responsibility and leadership on paper but unpacks these concepts throughout the curriculum and beyond?

The application of such virtues and an understanding of acting responsibly requires future leaders to know and understand themselves first in order to be able to change. Developing and cultivating self-awareness needs to be embedded in business school education strategies if what is proclaimed and stated in bold on so many business school websites is what we believe in and what we teach. It is a misconception that if we get the strategy right the rest follows (Waterman Jr, 1982). In fact, a deeper look at programme structures of mainstream undergraduate and postgraduate business school curriculums shows they do not reflect the schools' business education strategies, with minor exceptions, but research is scarce in this area (Grassl, 2012; Parilla et al., 2023). Little or no space is given to development and cultivation of self explicitly.

How we perceive ourselves and others and how we are perceived as leaders lies in our ability to connect with mind and body. If we only lead from the head but exclude our heart and do not listen to the gut, our decisions and ways of leading will be mechanical, transactional, and mindless-kindless acts of labour. We cannot lead responsibly without compassion and love for ourselves and others. We cannot lead responsibly without knowing and understanding our desires and hindrances and without learning how to manage these. We cannot lead responsibly in a state of suffering, consumed by judgment and envy. Only if we know ourselves deeply, know our fears, know who we are, how we respond in the present moment, can we act responsibly and truthfully. Paving the way for our future leaders starts with setting an intention for a business education strategy that is informed, driven, and underpinned by mindfulness as a concept, philosophy, and learning and teaching approach. The tools of meditation, breath work, yoga, journaling, and coaching should be integrated into business education at all levels to support this journey of exploration of self.

We have a choice to teach business knowledge and practice with or without compassion, kindness, and love. It is quite simple, and yet it seems too difficult to articulate on a piece of paper. The first step towards a mindfulness-driven business education strategy is to make that choice about what underpins learning, teaching, and scholarship in the business school, then set an intention.

9.2 Developing a business education strategy with intention and discernment

Developing an education strategy is challenging because it needs to be broad enough to have reach and last for several years. Centring the strategy around mindfulness by sprinkling mindfulness words over the document is likely to ignite scepticism, reduce trust, and be perceived as hot air. It would not do the power of mindfulness justice and would most likely be ridiculed. Instead, the benefits, the concepts, and the philosophy of mindfulness need to be connected with the 'big' problems businesses face and how business education could address these through developing future leaders who speak, act, and think in a way that alleviates suffering. Everything is interconnected. The way the business school community behaves, thinks, and feels translates into learning, teaching, and student experience. For instance, if a business school wanted to develop future leaders who are agile, able to cope with uncertainty, or have a sustainability and ethical mindset, then business schools themselves need to practise and model such behaviours.

Therefore, a mindfulness-driven business education strategy requires a holistic approach. It starts with a clear intention of what it is the business school cares about, and it commits to change. A first step towards setting an intention is to identify the themes and values a business school is most concerned with and eager to address, whether it is sustainability, responsibility, the ability to deal with uncertainty through agile management (Greiser et al., 2018), or developing social, emotional, and ethical future leaders (Mind and Life Education Research Network et al., 2012; Roeser & Peck, 2009). The next step is to connect the intention with mindfulness concepts.

Mindfulness approaches have been found to be invaluable in dealing with and managing uncertainty (Jacobs & Blustein, 2008) as they provide a basis for approaching uncertainty with clarity, calmness, and openness (Spinelli et al., 2023). Openness implies readiness for change, a variable that has been found to positively impact student social, emotional, and ethical development in business school classrooms (Karali et al., 2023). Mindful reflexivity is another tool proposed by management scholars (Burton et al., 2021) as a foundational model for managing uncertainty and increasing responsible management practices because mindfulness predicts moral responsibility (Small & Lew, 2021, p. 112):

> … a person who is mindful, and therefore acts with awareness, and remains observant, non-reactive, describing and non-judging in situations that require moral reasoning will also be morally responsible. … we can predict that a mindful person will not be likely to use euphemisms, distortions of consequences, attribution of blame to others or similar moral disengagement strategies when faced with ethical dilemmas.

Devising a mindfulness driven business education strategy requires agreement, understanding, and commitment from all stakeholders, with clear and implementable actions that goes beyond pure business knowledge transfer of productivity, profitability, and efficiency to business competence development (Bratianu et al., 2020; Clegg et al., 2013).

9.3 Adopting mindfulness language

I reviewed over one hundred business education strategies from a range of business schools globally to identify how mindfulness is mentioned implicitly and or explicitly as part of vision, mission statements, educational goals, values, strategies, and approaches. My analysis revealed that most business schools with specific education strategies feature commitment to building a better more just and kind world, so there is an underlying desire for mindful ways of working, collaborating, leading, and managing. But none are explicitly linked to mindfulness concepts. Mindfulness language is not incorporated into business education strategy yet. However, it is fair to say there are facets or certain mindfulness energies that one notices that indicate its presence, but again they feel more like hot air. Below is a list of vision and mission statements commonly found in business schools' education documents deduced from my analysis. The sad truth is that most business schools and education strategies use the same wording there is no distinction or differentiation, it is a copy and paste approach.

- Developing individuals to become highly competent, socially responsible, and morally upright leaders.
- Empowering learners to take responsibility.
- Inspiring our students and using holistic approaches to learning and teaching that develop open mindedness and inclusive thinking.
- Graduates are distinguished not just by knowledge but by their wisdom, character, service ethic, and global mindset.
- Enabling future leaders to act with integrity.
- Our students are encouraged to listen and respond to the needs of others and the environment.
- Develop and promote resourcefulness in our students.
- Inspire brilliant minds to be the world's future leaders of business and society.
- Support graduates to become curious, creative, and resilient individuals, who are well placed to serve as socially and environmentally responsible citizens, managers, and leaders.
- Develop future leaders who are adaptable and resilient.
- Empowering our communities to apply business knowledge for positive societal impact.
- Develop employable graduates who add value to their constituent communities and society at large.

The snapshot of the statements predominantly used by business schools as opening statements of their education strategy highlights that as a community of educators, we share the same vision, but there are two questions that arise. First, does the business education we provide really reflect that, is it a true representation? Second, are we as educators committed to delivering it and equipped to do so?

From my experience of working with business schools to devise mindfulness driven education portfolios, the cookie-cutter approach taken to create business education strategies is easy and cheap. Ready-made, off-the-shelf business education strategies are quick to produce and implement as a box-ticking exercise, yet they are built on the same old ideas of capitalism and productivity resulting in the creation of 'egosystem' leaders (Blakstad et al., 2018) the opposite of what a mindfulness-driven business education approach endeavours to do. Crocker et al. (2008) distinguish between egosystem and ecosystem goals that determine one's approach to solving problems, managing a business, or in this case, providing business education. Egosystem goals refer to self-oriented needs that are rooted in thoughts of scarcity and entitlement to some extent. Egosystem goals enable an individual to maintain a certain desired self-image that only serves the individual. In contrast, ecosystem goals are considered goals that serve a system of individuals, and these goals have an impact on others both positive and negative. Whether one adopts an egosystem or ecosystem goal approach depends on how the relationship with self and others has been established in the first place through social environments including education.

We need an awareness paradigm shift in business schools that embraces the break from same old, same old, traditional, reductionist-thinking, egosystems awareness to a co-created, value-driven, and holistic ecosystems awareness (Blakstad et al., 2018; Scharmer & Kaufer, 2013; Zu, 2022). With that in mind, we can be clear about what kind of world we want to create before we start writing a strategy, and it all starts with intention.

A business education strategy can be understood as a functional strategy (Bora et al., 2017) within the strategy pyramid widely known and used in the context of business strategy development. Its position therefore within a wider school or even institutional strategy adds layers of complexity to what might be possible, of course, but within the constraints there is usually room for manoeuvre. Even though, a business school might be restricted by university-wide educational benchmarks, in my experience, there is room for adding a unique perspective. I have also found that business schools have influence and are often pioneers in devising innovative education approaches that are often adopted by the wider university. Therefore, I would encourage senior leaders in business schools to be bold and push back against wider university educational strategies if they appear to prevent the development of a mindfulness driven approach to business education.

9.4 Foundations of mindfulness and business education strategy

In Chapter 1, I introduced the four foundations of mindfulness known as the *satipatthana*: (1) mindfulness of the body, (2) mindfulness of feeling tone, (3) mindfulness of mental states and (4) mindfulness of our experience of the world. We can apply those foundations to devise a business education strategy that is guided and underpinned by mindfulness instead of just sprinkling it on top. Similar to most corporate business strategies, education strategies are built on six elements: vision, mission, objectives/goals, strategies, approach/methodology, and tactics/action plans. The vision, mission and goals are understood as the cornerstones of an educational institution and guide operational processes and procedures such as approaches, tactics, and actions (Parilla et al., 2023).

Business schools as body and systems – mindfulness of the body

A business school can be understood as a body, an ecosystem with physical, mental, emotional, and energetic states of being, values, and a set of skills. As such our vision and mission should reflect our ecosystem mission, vision, goals, values, methods, and ways of doing. The vision should be an aspiration, a short statement that reflects what the business education provided wants to achieve in the long term and what one can expect from studying at a particular business school. The mission statement refers to the initial educational idea of a particular business school. It might mention the founders and their original thought around the purpose of providing business education. This aspect is a lot harder for most business schools because a lot of business schools are young and have seen many deans come and go. Thus, the 'body/system' has changed continuously over time, and it is not uncommon for business schools to lose their sense of purpose and who they are in the process. In fact, some business schools thrive on their leadership, and there is fear and uncertainty about what might happen if a specific dean leaves, as the person is part of the schools identity, purpose, and educational mission. It is not surprising therefore that business schools might struggle to formulate and develop an educational strategy if they have lost their purpose (Koris et al., 2017). Perhaps there is also a misconception about what purpose is: 'Purpose is definitely not some jargon-filled catch-all … it doesn't have to be aspirational or cause-based … it is who you cannot help being.; (Craig & Snook, 2014). The latter point seems crucial in the context of developing a business education strategy as, if business schools know who they 'cannot help being,' it might enable them to be more authentic in their statements. More often than not business schools try to be something they are not. The questions below can kick start this process of understanding a business school's purpose as a system/body:

1. Who are we now?
2. Who do we want to be?
3. What does the business school body pay attention to and what not?

4. How does the business school body breathe or not? Where is tightness and where is space in the system to grow?
5. What do we need to create an environment that reflects our aspirations, values, and skills?
6. Who do we need and want to work with?
7. What concepts and framework serve our vision and mission?
8. What business education reflects our vision and mission?
9. What are our fears if we step outside the cookie cutter approach?

Find a space to explore these questions. It might take a while and give your body/system permission to let whatever comes up arise, observe, witness, and be non-judgmental in the process. Utilise your body wisely and draw on how the different parts of the body (staff and students) respond. If we ignore the body's ways of speaking and communicating, the body has no choice but become ill, and this is often reflected in a toxic culture. The body simply says no (Maté, 2011), and the response is decay, illness, and suffering. The first foundation, mindfulness of the body, can be a helpful mechanism to start the process of developing a vision, mission, and purpose statement for a mindfulness-driven business education strategy.

Egosystem versus ecosystem goals – Mindfulness of feeling tone

In the process of answering the questions above, remain open to how the process feels. Some answers might be unpleasant, some pleasant. Some answers might call for behaviour change, such as to evoke a paradigm shift from egosystem to ecosystem awareness, from top-down hierarchical leadership to system, contemplative leadership. Perhaps it requires a restructure of departments and letting go of people who are not aligned with the new vision, mission, and purpose. In my experience, this process is a push and pull between excitement and exhaustion, between the tenacity and passion to change and constant evaluation of the risk and the resources required. It is a lot harder and more complex to adopt an ecosystem approach because it inherently means being compassionate. Working with feeling tone is all about compassion towards the body's/system's needs. Reflection and returning to the questions above in an iterative way can diffuse that push and pull, which, if ongoing, can create unhealthy imbalance in the system. Hence, high staff turnover is perceived as disruptive and out of balance. At the same time as this state of imbalance exists, it is necessary to learn to be *okay* with the unpleasant, but also with what is neutral and pleasant, whether it is ideas or decisions surrounding the development of the strategy.

Once the vision and mission are agreed at a first level, identifying objectives that are aligned with the mindful approach can guide the next steps. Ecosystem goals are based on the idea that the needs of a group are interconnected, and actions have an impact on others. For instance, if staff and students learn that meditations reduce anxiety, and they experience the benefits as part of a group session, they are more likely to suggest meditation as a tool to peers or later to colleagues at work. We can refer to these as social outcomes that are created by people through sharing and giving to others, which increases wellbeing (Crocker, 2008). At this point the concern is less about self-image than genuine care for others, which is expressed through compassion, support, and generosity. However, it is worth noting that future leaders need to develop both, egosystem and ecosystem goals and they need to be able to comfortably switch from one to another. Egosystem goals are related to increased energy and high motivation, which is important to drive innovation and manage large complex projects. Success, recognition, and admiration are the fruits of the energy invested based on these types of goals. Yet, it is a short-lived event, because when the ego quiets so do motivation, enthusiasm, and passion because the goal was extrinsically motivated. Ecosystem goals prioritise self and others and are intrinsically motivated, which can still include passion and commitment. The focal point is not the self but the system surrounding the self and how well the system functions. Therefore, people with ecosystem goals have been found to learn more and develop themselves further because they are driven by the need to support others, which in turn improves their relationships too. Jiang et al. (2023) introduced the term compassionate goals as a way to define ecosystem awareness and goals at a deeper level. Participants in the study, who set compassionate goals felt more secure and trusted and had better quality relationships. In fact, compassionate goals helped participants forge good relationships despite insecurities.

Thus, business schools, as a system, need to consider both egosystem and ecosystem goals but with an emphasis on compassion. The importance is to help those parts of the system, academics and students to name primary stakeholders, to be aware of both and how to utilise them as part of their learning, teaching, and scholarship. Perhaps egosystem goals can relate to the individuals in the system, but they can still be compassionate in nature, self-compassion for instance. Whereas ecosystem goals are aimed at impact beyond the self and promote responsive behaviour in both good and bad times (Jiang et al., 2023). The following questions might be helpful in developing system goals for a mindfulness-driven business education strategy:

Egosystem goals with compassion

1. What is important to me? Is it power, recognition, enjoyment, or to be the cash cow?
2. Why is it important?
3. What are my needs to deliver outstanding learning, teaching, and scholarship/What are my needs to provide the effective leadership required?
4. How does it feel to know what is important to me and to be clear about what I need?

5. Formulate three goals in alignment with the above. They can be self-oriented and serve the body's needs only.
6. How do these fit with the business education strategy developed so far?

Ecosystem goals with compassion

1. What is it important for the business school to achieve?
2. Why is it important?
3. Identify three goals that align with the vision and mission set out so far.
4. How does it feel? Why does it feel pleasant, neutral or unpleasant?
5. What would you like to change to better serve the system?

Edward Taylor, Vice Provost and Dean of Undergraduate Academic Affairs at the University of Washington, US, shared in a Mind & Life podcast in April 2023 (Hasenkamp & Taylor, 2023present). how he and colleagues used an ecosystem awareness and compassionate goal setting approach to bring students back to campus after the pandemic restrictions. It is a great example of its application at scale and testament to its power and impact. Students reported high levels of anxiety about returning to campus in person. In collaboration with the resilience lab, Taylor and colleagues created a public forum to talk about resilience, compassion, care, and mindfulness on campus. The high levels of anxiety among students is a system problem. They asked themselves how to become an institution of care and how to become a place that is committed to developing habits of mind and heart so everyone could come back as a community. To address the question, a committee of staff and students was created with the purpose of crafting messages that reflect resilience, compassion, mind, and heart on campus and to distribute these through students. Co-creation was the strategy because, in their conversations with students, they learned that students listen to each other but delete emails from academics. Becoming an institution of care is an ecosystem and compassionate goal. It is positioned in the present moment and reflects what matters, what is important to the educational body. We can harness the power of now (Tolle, 2004).

Strategies, approaches, and tactics to adopt a new mindset and behaviours in business education – Mindfulness of mind

We have established throughout the book that business schools have a responsibility to develop future leaders in various ways, and I offered a range of different tools to shape their relationships, particularly the relationship with our self, our thoughts, and emotions. While we can implement those tools at different levels, the way we, as education providers, think about them and communicate them through various channels is central to their success and impact, and the same is true of the strategies we choose to shape the mindset of the system. The strategies, approaches, tactics, and actions we formulate are an expression of our thoughts. However, if we only focus on what already exists and has been created, we are unable to see beyond that. I don't feel that, on a conceptual level, we are a million miles away from creating a mindfulness-driven business education strategy, but we have not mastered translating our thoughts and words into reality yet so they can truly change our learning and teaching practice.

Business education providers offer a range of programmes at undergraduate, postgraduate, and executive level. The nature of the programmes and any extracurricular offerings must be aligned with the vision, mission, and goals set out above. For instance, to develop self-aware and compassionate future leaders, the strategy might be to engage students and staff in co-creation of knowledge, learning, and experience, to provide a space for growth, social interaction, collaboration, and reflection. Both examples take an ecosystem perspective but also allow egosystem goals to be addressed. A space for growth might be a physical or a virtual space, in the classroom or outside the classroom. The specifics need to be aligned and implemented in such a way that they can be measured and, at some point, evaluated. Outlining the approach in detail will mean taking time to explore the depths of the mind of our business school body and all its parts.

If co-creation is a central point of the business education strategy, a review of existing services, mainly programmes, is needed, from learning aims and outcomes to assessments, content, and learning and teaching methods. This part is often neglected as it is cumbersome. Yet programmes are the bread and butter of business schools and business schools are an integral part of an institution's economic health. How we teach, what we teach, and who teaches influences the minds of future leaders because we constantly share thoughts, concepts, and ideas. In addition to reviewing existing services, I recommend considering the following aspects too: product/service, people, culture and image. Below are questions to explore these aspects further:

1. *Service:*
    - How do programmes reflect the new vision and mission?
    - What thoughts, concepts and ideas do they communicate?
    - How do these translate into the operational processes of the programme both academically and administratively?

2. *People:*
    - Who is delivering the programmes?
    - How aligned are those delivering the programmes with the mindfulness-driven education approach? Do they have to be and, if so, to what extent or, if not, why not?

- What approaches and tactics can we use to equip educators with the relevant knowledge and skills to deliver the new vision and mission?

3. *Culture:*
   - What are the thoughts and behaviour underpinning and driving the mindfulness-driven business education strategy at a cultural level?
   - How and what would we need to change?
   - What approaches and tactics would foster adoption of an aligned mindset and behaviours?

4. *Image:*
   - How do we want to be perceived externally?
   - Who do we want to engage with outside who align with the new vision and mission?
   - What approaches and tactics are helpful in communicating the new image? What thoughts and ideas strengthen and nurture or weaken the new image?

The questions above are simply to kick-start the conversation, to enable new ways of thinking about how we can move from one mindset to another way of thinking, another perspective that leads to the creation of new behaviours. This shift in mindset and behaviour is about making choices. These choices are intentional, deliberate, and conscious in nature. The choices we make today have an impact on our future leaders, and as business educators and those that shape strategy, we are at the epicentre of making decisions that can either lead to great gain or suffering (Karelaia & Reb, 2015).

We might believe that we can only change history through scholarship and research, but we can change and make history through our choices around learning and teaching with or without mindfulness in mind.

Evaluating the lived experience – Mindfulness of *Dharma*

A developing education strategy is a mental model, a mental representation of what we think is right. It speaks one truth that must last for three, five, or ten years. Rarely, unless a new dean is appointed, do we go back and interrogate our strategy, question whether we are still truthful in our thoughts and actions because if we do not evaluate our strategy regularly, we are very likely to experience suffering. Obstacles are part of life and in higher education, we are not immune to the geopolitical, social, and economic changes that lead to most of the suffering on our planet. Obstacles and hindrances are external events, mostly outside our control and certainly not considered in education strategy documents. Such obstacles might be a decline in student numbers, reduced student engagement, an increase in mental health challenges, an increase in chronic diseases resulting in staff absences, limited access to research funding, an increase in staff costs ... the list is endless. Even with a well-devised business education strategy including ecosystem and compassionate goals, it is those obstacles that can easily lead to a relapse; pushing a system from ecosystem awareness back to an egosystem awareness. In this state the five hindrances, desire, aversion, sloth and torpor, restlessness and worry, and doubt, infiltrate the body, the culture, and structure of the system resulting in imbalance. A system built on a strategy that only exists on paper as a concept but is not a lived experience is likely to fold. So, the question to ask again and again is: Are we still true to ourselves, true to what we set out and proclaimed and, if not, how can we change that?

The desire for change will become louder and louder as suffering gains momentum. Aversion towards initiatives is one of those signs, accompanied by pessimism, disbelief, low confidence, and doubt. Sloth and torpor, restlessness and worry spread like fire throughout the system. Understanding the value and power of the fourth foundation of mindfulness and how to use it as a tool to evaluate not just the suffering but the direction of the business education path we envisage can alleviate the suffering. The eightfold path as part of our experience can bring clarity and compassion to suffering and enrich learning and teaching in business schools at their core.

Efforts should be made to regularly evaluate and assess the perception, congruency, and application of the business education strategy in the school. This approach increases acceptance, awareness, and understanding among stakeholders through clarity and consistency (Parilla et al., 2023). Such evaluation includes listening to and observation and noticing of lived experience through asking the questions outlined above again and again and again. Peter Drucker once warned, 'The most serious mistakes are not being made as a result of wrong answers. The truly dangerous thing is asking the wrong questions' (Drucker, 2010). The questions might seem obvious and simple, but the answers are all choices that can have a profound impact on the future of learning and teaching in business schools, the student experience, and long-term implications for how graduates behave, think, and feel as future leaders and managers.

Chapter 9 in a nutshell...

A mindfulness-driven business education strategy has the power to change history. The way we share business and management theories, concepts, and thoughts with students in business schools shapes future leaders' thoughts, emotions, and actions. We are in charge, we have the power to make change happen, to prevent and reverse an egosystem society, to become an ecosystem, compassionate community that cares about people and the planet instead of profit and productivity.

Applying the four foundations of mindfulness to business education strategy development enables us to perceive and understand the implications of our thoughts, emotions, and actions at a different level. Mindfulness of the body – business schools are bodies and each body, is a system. How the body feels, moves, perceives, and breathes depends on how we treat it, feed it, and nurture it.

Mindfulness of feeling tone – the body, the system, experiences emotions that are shared with every single part of it inside, felt by every single part of it inside. Some are pleasant, some are neutral, and some are unpleasant. Creating balance of feeling tone within the system can be achieved by setting ecosystem and compassionate goals so that unpleasantness becomes an opportunity to learn and change.

Mindfulness of the mind – the strategies, tactics and actions we chose to deploy in our classrooms and accompanying thoughts shape our students. Our choices of sharing certain management theories and concepts or not and how we position and portray them influences the minds of our future leaders.

Mindfulness of *Dharma*/experience – Developing a strategy is not hard, but remembering to apply strategic thinking and decision making in a mindful way is (does that statement sound familiar?), and as with anything we want to change, practice and evaluation are the key to positive change.

I would like to close this final chapter with the following adapted Verse 67, 'Compassion,' from the *Tao Te Ching* (Tzu, 2021), which I believe summarises what I have said above about how to think about devising a mindfulness-driven business education strategy and might even function as a list of virtues for our community:

> When a person puts on a show, Trying to appear great,
> Their mediocrity is soon exposed. Three treasures, the wise guard and cherish: The first is compassion, The second is economy, The third is humility.
> If you are compassionate, you can be truly courageous. If you are economical, you can be truly generous. If you are humble, you can be truly helpful.
> If you are brave but lack compassion, Are generous but lack economy, and try to help others but lack humility, You have lost the way.

References

Blakstad, S., & Allen, R. (2018). Ecosystem vs egosystem and revolution vs evolution. In Blakstad, S., & Allen, R. (Eds.) *FinTech revolution: Universal inclusion in the new financial ecosystem* (pp. 3–17). Springer.

Blass, E., & Hayward, P. (2015). Developing globally responsible leaders: What role for business schools in the future? *Futures*, 66, 35–44.

Bora, B., Borah, S., & Chungyalpa, W. (2017). Crafting strategic objectives: Examining the role of business vision and mission statements. *Journal of Entrepreneurship & Organization Management*, 6(1), 1–6.

Bratianu, C., Hadad, S., & Bejinaru, R. (2020). Paradigm shift in business education: a competence-based approach. *Sustainability*, 12(4), 1348.

Burton, N., Culham, T., & Vu, M. C. (2021). Spiritual practice and management education pedagogy: Exploring the philosophical foundations of three spiritual traditions. *Journal of Management Education*, 45(2), 206–242. https://doi.org/10.1177/1052562920945739.

Clegg, S. R., Jarvis, W. P., & Pitsis, T. S. (2013). Making strategy matter: Social theory, knowledge interests and business education. *Business History*, 55(7), 1247–1264.

Craig, N., & Snook, S. (2014). From purpose to impact. *Harvard Business Review*, 92(5), 104–111.

Crocker, J. (2008). *From egosystem to ecosystem: Implications for relationships, learning, and well-being.*

Crocker, J., Breines, J. G., Canevello, A., Liu, M. Y., & Niiya, Y. (2008). Egosystem and ecosystem goals and adjustment to college. In H. Marsh, R. G. Craven, & D. M. McInerney (Eds.), *Self-processes, Learning, and Enabling Human Potential: Dynamic New Approaches* (pp. 251–268). Information Age Publishing.

Drucker, P. F. (2010). *Men, ideas, and politics*. Harvard Business Press.

Grassl, W. (2012). Mission, vision, strategy: Discernment in Catholic business education. *Journal of Catholic Higher Education*, 31(2), 213–232.

Greiser, C., Martini, J.-P. & Meissner, N. (2018). *Unleashing the power of mindfulness in corporations*. The Boston Consulting Group (BCG). https://web-assets.bcg.com/cc/db/b39118d84b34be612fe22194f646/unleashing-the-power-of-mindfulness-in-corporations-rev.pdf.

Hasenkamp, W. & Taylor, E. (Hosts). (2023–present). *Ed Taylor – Leading by Example* [Audio podcast]. Mind & Life. https://podcast.mindandlife.org/ed-taylor/.

Jacobs, S. J., & Blustein, D. L. (2008). Mindfulness as a coping mechanism for employment uncertainty. *The Career Development Quarterly*, 57(2), 174–180.

Jiang, T., Canevallo, A., & Crocker, J. (2023). Compassionate goals, responsiveness, and well-being. *Current Opinion in Psychology*, 52, 101634. https://doi.org/10.1016/j.copsyc.2023.101634.

Karali, N., Mastrokoukou, S., & Livas, C. (2023). Mindful minds and entrepreneurial spirits in higher education: A scoping review. *Frontiers in Education*, 8, 1–17. https://doi.org/10.3389/feduc.2023.1291845.

Karelaia, N., & Reb, J. (2015). Improving decision making through mindfulness. In J. Reb, & P. W. B. Atkins (Eds.), *Mindfulness in organizations: Foundations, research, and applications*, 163–187.

Koris, R., Örtenblad, A., & Ojala, T. (2017). From maintaining the status quo to promoting free thinking and inquiry: Business students' perspective on the purpose of business school teaching. *Management Learning*, 48(2), 174–186.

Lorange, P. (2005). Strategy means choice: Also for today's business school! *Journal of Management Development*, 24(9), 783–790. https://doi.org/10.1108/02621710510621295.

Maté, G. (2011). *When the body says no: The cost of hidden stress*. Vintage.

Mind and Life Education Research Network, Davidson, R. J., Dunne, J., Eccles, J. S., Engle, A., Greenberg, M., Jennings, P., Jha, A., Jinpa, T., & Lantieri, L. (2012). Contemplative practices and mental training: Prospects for American education. *Child Development Perspectives*, 6(2), 146–153.

Osiemo, L. B. (2012). Developing responsible leaders: The university at the service of the person. *Journal of Business Ethics*, 108, 131–143.

Parilla, E. S., Abadilla, M. E., Tan, J. P., & Domingo, G. (2023). Understanding, acceptance, and perception of the vision, mission, goals, and objectives of the Northwestern University College of Business Education stakeholders. *Education Policy and Development*, 1(1). 33–49.

Roeser, R. W., & Peck, S. C. (2009). An education in awareness: Self, motivation, and self-regulated learning in contemplative perspective. *Educational Psychologist*, 44(2), 119–136.

Scharmer, O., & Kaufer, K. (2013). *Leading from the emerging future: From ego-system to eco-system economies.* Berrett-Koehler Publishers.

Small, C., & Lew, C. (2021). Mindfulness, moral reasoning and responsibility: Towards virtue in ethical decision-making. *Journal of business ethics*, 169(1), 103–117.

Spinelli, C., Ibrahim, M., & Khoury, B. (2023). Cultivating ambiguity tolerance through mindfulness: An induction randomized controlled trial. *Current Psychology*, 42(15), 12929–12947.

Tolle, E. (2004). *The power of now: A guide to spiritual enlightenment.* New World Library.

Tzu, L. (2021). *Tao Te Ching. The book of the way.* Ancient Renewal.

Waterman Jr, R. H. (1982). The seven elements of strategic fit. *The Journal of Business Strategy*, 2(3), 69.

Zu, L. (2022). Changing your system, changing the world: From ego-system to eco-system. In *Responsible and sustainable business: The Taoism's perspective* (pp. 19–23). Springer.

INDEX

Page numbers in *italics* denote figures, those in **bold** denote tables.

AACSB *see* American Association of Collegiate Schools of Business
absence, mental 44, 46
absenteeism 58–59
academic achievement 104
academic engagement 104
acceptance/self-acceptance 53, 73, 76, 93–96, 142
accountability 33
active learning 43–44
Acton, R. M. 25
Adhia, H. 59
affirmations 80, 81, 122
aggregates of clinging (*khandhas*) 18, 19
agility 30, 133
alternate nostril breathing 91
ambiguity 28, 30
American Association of Collegiate Schools of Business (AACSB) 24–25, 62
American business schools 24–25
Amoroso, L. M. 102
Angelo, J. 91
anxiety 17, 18, 27, 42, 80–81, 116
appreciation 15–16, 116–117
Ardelt, M. 111
Arranz, N. 73
artificial intelligence (AI) 62–64, 65
artificial super intelligence (ASI) 64
assessment of mindfulness skills 110–113; poster presentation 110–111; reflective and prospective account 111–113

Asthana, A. N. 47, 85
Atkins, P. W. 9
attendance, extracurricular activities 71–72
attention 13, 26, 27, 28, 52
attentiveness 53
attitude 26, 27, 28
Australia 72
authenticity, cultivation of 47
aversion 17, 18, 96, 142
awareness intelligence 3, 8, 36, 63, 64, 87; *see also* emotional intelligence; self-awareness; somatic intelligence
Azman, A. W. 53

Baer, R. A. 45, 47
Bakhshandeh, B. 117
balancing breath 91
Bartkus, K. R. 71
Bathurst, R. 35
Baumeister, R. F. 112
Bautista, T. 61
Bennis, W. G. 26, 29
The Bhagavad Gita (Easwaran) 54, 65, 112–113
Bishop, K. 45–46
Black Lives Matter 61
Blake, A. 35, 93
Blakstad, S. 135
blame 17, 133
Blass, E. 131, 132
Bloom, B. S. 13

Bloom, S. G. 52
Blustein, D. L. 133
bodily wisdom 35
bodily-kinaesthetic intelligence 64
body 33; mindfulness of 14–16, 29–30, 86–90, 135, 136–137, 143
body part contemplation 15–16
body scan 15, 87, 88–89, 124, 126
body—mind dichotomy 35
Boone, L. E. 73
Bora, B. 135
Borker, D. R. 42, 43
Bowden, J. L.-H. 46
Boyatzis, R. E. 81, 82
Brantley, J. 9
Bratianu, C. 133
breath work 15, 16, 87–88, 116, 119, 124, 126
breathing 16, 27, 30, 89; alternate nostril 91; balancing breath 91; qualities of 16
Brewer, J. A. 80
Brink, E. 59, 60
Brinkmann, A. E. 59
Brodbeck, F. C. 81–82
Bronk, K. C. 112
brown eye/blue eye exercise 52
Brown, K. W. 9, 46
Bruce, K. 25
Bryant, S. M. 25
Buddha/Buddhism 8, 13, 14, 21, 26, 27, 43, 82; *see also* foundations of mindfulness
Burke, M. 102
burnout 58–59
Burton, N. 41, 42, 43, 44, 45, 49, 133
business education, mindfulness and *see* mindfulness and business education
business education strategy 131–145; adoption of mindfulness language 134–135; co-creation and 131, 139, 140; cultural level aspects 141; elements 136; evaluating the lived experience of 141–142; foundations of mindfulness and 135–142, 143; image and 141; intention and discernment and development of 132–133; people considerations 140–141; product/service aspects 140
business schools: accreditation 25; mission statements 134–135, 136, 137; origin and development of 24–25; practice-oriented versus theory-based teaching 25, 26; purpose 136–137; rankings 25; responsibility 131–132; as system/body 136–137; vision 134, 136, 137

Cahn, B. R. 59
Cain, T. 35
capitalism 20–21
care 139; pedagogy of 52–53, 54; *see also* self-care
career management 102, 103
Carey, W. 116
Carnegie Foundation 25
Carruthers, C. 9
Celoria, D. 117
CEOs 28, 85
Chiang, E. P. 42, 46
chocolate meditation 91–92
clarifying 119, 125
clarity 30, 133
Clegg, S. R. 131, 133
climate change/climate adaption 59–60
clinging, aggregates of (*khandhas*) 18, 19
co-creation 85–86, 100, 135; business education strategy 131, 139, 140; extracurricular mindfulness sessions 82
coaching 50, 51; in business education 117–118; peer 117; person-oriented approach 117, 118, 127; traditional models 118; *see also* mindfulness coaching
codes of conduct and ethics 51
cognitive availability 53
cognitive domains 13
commitment, and extracurricular activities 71–72
comparison 79
compassion 61–62, 63, 65, 108, 118, 138, 143; ecosystem goals with 139; egosystem goals with 138–139; self-compassion 76, 138
compassionate goals 138–139, 142, 143
complexity 28, 30
complexity mindset 30
Compte, O. 116
concentration 20, 29, 52, 72, 89
conceptual self-awareness 35
confidence 53, 116, 117, 118, 122
conscientiousness 47
contemplative leadership 33, 34, 36
contemplative pedagogy 52, 54
contemplative pedagogy centres 52
contracted (constricted) mind 94
Corti, L. 118, 126
Cotton, D. R. 62
Covid pandemic 61, 139
Craig, N. 136
Crocker, J. 135, 138
Culham, T. E. 41, 52

culture, and business education strategy 141
Cunliffe, A. 43

Datta, R. 18
Davis, K. 63, 64
Dean, K. L. 51
decision making 47; and emotions/emotional states 42, 44; ethical 42–43, 44, 54; and System 1 and System 2 thinking 42
DEI *see* diversity, equity, and inclusion
dependent arising 43
desire 18, 54, 63, 96, 112–113, 142
Dharma (*Dhammas*), mindfulness of 18–20, **20**, 63, 86, 97–99, 104–105, 141–142, 143
disadvantage 61
discretion 53
dispositional mindfulness 46
distortion: of experience 105; of the mind 105; of perception 105
distracted mind 44, 46, 94–95
Diver, A. 106
diversity, equity, and inclusion (DEI) 61–62, 65
Donham, W. B. 25, 29
Doty, J. R. 52
doubt 18, 19, 63, 96, 116, 142
Dries, N. 103
Drucker, P. F. 142
Dweck, C. S. 108

Easwaran, E., *The Bhagavad Gita* 54, 65, 112–113
ecosystem goals 135, 137–138, 140, 142, 143; with compassion 139
effectiveness of mindfulness in business classroom 46–48
ego desires 18
egosystem goals 135, 137–138, 140; with compassion 138–139
eightfold path 20, 142
Elkington, J. 21
Elsey, E. L. 89, 90
embodied leadership 33, 35–36
embodied perception 35
embodied practice 34
embodied self-awareness 35, 36
emotional availability 53
emotional intelligence 36, 44–46, 54, 59, 63, 106
emotional self-awareness 106
emotions/emotional states 17–18, 33, 49; and decision making 42, 44; regulation of 42, 44, 46, 47–48, 52, 111

empathy 44, 53, 63
employability 32, 72, 84, 102, 120, 123, 134
employee wellbeing 58–59, 65
empty meditation 94
engagement, student *see* student engagement
Engleman-Lampe, C. 42
'Enrich Your Study Life' case study 85–99; Body, intention, and breathing workshop 86–90; Feelings and self-awareness workshop 86, 90–93; Hindrances and manifestation workshop 86, 96–99; Mind and self-acceptance workshop 76, 93–96
equity 61
Ergas, O. 26–28, 41, 48
Ericson, T. 59, 60
Eriksen, M. 117, 123
Ernst, J. 53
ethical blind spots 42
ethical decision making 42–43, 44, 54
ethics 53, 133; code of 51
Euchner, J. 29
Eurich, T. 35–36, 47, 123
expectations 19, 21, 75, 76, 77, 78, 80, 86–87, 112
experience, distortion of 105
experiential learning 43, 44, 51–52, 54, 117
external self-awareness 35, 36, 47, 59, 90, 93, 123, 125, 126
exteroception 35
extracurricular activities 71–83; benefits of 73; case study *see* 'Good Enough' mini retreat case study; engagement, commitment and attendance challenges 71–72, 73; incentives 73; length of programmes 73; student-led 73

facilitation *see* teaching mindfulness
fear 63; of judgment 77
Fedynich, L. 30
feeling tone: mindfulness of 16–17, 30, 86, 90–93, 135, 137–139, 143; of pleasantness, unpleasantness, and neutrality 91, 92
Feldman, C. 14, 17
Finland 73
Fisher, K. 35
Five Facets Mindfulness Questionnaire (FFMQ) 47
flipped classroom 44
Floyd, G. 61
Fogel, A. 35
Ford Foundation 25
foundations of mindfulness 14–20, 29–30, 81; and business education strategy

135–142, 143; mindfulness of the body 14–16, 29–30, 86–90, 135, 136–137, 143; mindfulness of *Dharma* 18–20, **20**, 63, 86, 97, 97–99, 104–105, 141–142, 143; mindfulness of feeling tone 16–17, 30, 86, 90–93, 135, 137–139, 143; mindfulness of mind 13–14, 17–18, 30, 86, 93–96, 136, 139–141, 143
Fox, K. C. 59
Frank, P. 60

Gajda, D. 59
Gammie, B. 102
Gan, G. 117, 126
Gardner, F. L. 9
Gardner, H. 64
Gardner, J. 62
Gay, E. F. 24
Gazzaley, A. 44
Gelati, C. 118, 126
Gelles, D. 9, 49, 58
generative mindfulness 62
generosity 34, 94, 138
Goldman Schuyler, K. 61, 62
Goldstein, J. 9, 13, 14, 18, 63, 74, 97
Goleman, D. 90, 106, 117
Gonzalez, M. 9
'Good Enough' mini retreat case study 73–83; coaching and journal time 74, 80–81; comparing and the inner critic 79; considerations 81–82; opening meditation 75–76; retreat structure **74**, 74–75; yoga sequence 76–80
good intentions 89
Goodman, M. S. 8
Gowan, M. A. 102
grades 104
Grandy, G. 34
Grant, P. 41, 43
Grassl, W. 132
gratitude 15–16, 116–117; inviting 79
gratitude journals 90
greed 54, 65, 94
Greiser, C. 133
group work 17, 97
Grunwald, S. 111
Gutterman, A. 30

Hadar, L. L. 26–28, 41, 48
Hall, D. T. 116
Hamill, P. 35
happiness 3, 60
Harajli, D. A. 42, 43, 45, 49
Harris, S. 33
Harvard Business School 24, 25

Hasenkamp, W. 139
Hayward, P. 131, 132
heart desires 18
Heineberg, Y. 81
Hemphill, D. 117
Herzberg, F. 73
Hibbert, P. 43
hindrances 18–20, 54, 63, 96–99, 141–142
Hitchcock, S. 72
Hogg, P. 62
holding space 53
Holland, A. 62, 64
Hollenbeck, G. P. 116
honesty 54, 90
Hood, C. D. 9
Hoomans, J. 42
Huang, M.-H. 63
human capital 131
humanised leadership 52, 53–54
humility 22
Hunt, T. 30

image, and business education strategy 141
impermanence 43, 92, 105
incentives, extracurricular activities 73
inclusive workplaces 61–62
information, hunger for 44
inner critic 79
integrity 22, 54
intelligence(s): as biopsychological potential 63; emotional 36, 44–46, 54, 59, 63, 106; somatic 35, 36, 63; theory of multiple intelligences 64; *see also* artificial intelligence (AI); awareness intelligence
intention(s) 13, 26, 27, 28, 86–87, 119; developing business education strategy with 132–133; good 89
internal self-awareness 35–36, 47, 59, 90, 93, 123–124, 125, 126
interoception 35
interpersonal intelligence 64
intrapersonal intelligence 64
intrinsic motivation 113, 114
introspection 18, 19, 28, 34, 80, 111
intuition 43, 48, 49
Isopahkala-Bouret, U. 73

Jacobs, S. J. 133
Jamison, D. 102
Jane Elliott's Brown Eye/Blue Eye Test 52
Jennings, N. 104
Jiang, T. 138
Johansen, B. 29
journaling 45, 74, 80, 89–90, 125

judgment, fear of 77

Kabatt-Zinn, J. 3, 28, 60
Kahneman, D. 42
Karali, N. 133
Karelaia, N. 141
Kaufer, K. 135
Kay, A. A. 47
Kentucky Inventory of Mindfulness Skills 45
khandhas (aggregates of clinging) 18, 19
kindness 22, 118; love and kindness exercises 48
King, A. S. 26, 30
Klitmøller, A. 53
Klug, K. 108
knowledge 13, 49; self-knowledge 49, 111, 124
Kohls, N. 104
Koris, R. 136
Koyenikan, I. 13
Krägeloh, C. 62
Krishnan, H. A. 33, 85
Kuechler, W. 42, 43
Kuyken, W. 14, 17

Lam, G. 108
Lampe, M. 42
Langer, E. J. 8
Lawrence, E. 106
Lawrence, K. 29
leadership 30–33, 81–82, 131–132; contemplative 33, 34, 36; embodied 33, 35–36; historical aspects of 32; humanised 52, 53–54; periods, eras, and schools of thought 30, **31**; relational 35; skills development 32–33; traits 32
learning: active 43–44; experiential 43, 44, 51–52, 54, 117
'learning by presence' 33
Leggett, R. 122, 125
Lemisiou, M. A. 117, 126
Lew, C. 133
Libri, V. 116
life management 104
Lim, H. J. 59
linguistic intelligence 64
listening 29, 117, 119, 125
Liu, Z. 117
Lock, D. A. 106
Locke, E. A. 25
Lorange, P. 131
love and kindness exercises 48
Lowitz, L. 18

MAAS (Mindful Attention Awareness Scale) 45, 46
Malinowski, P. 59
mark release time 73, 74
Marques, J. F. 9, 41
Martin, D. 82
Maté, G. 137
mathematical intelligence 64
Mayer, D. 112
MBA students 85; *see also* 'Enrich Your Study Life' case study
MBCT (mindfulness based cognitive therapy) 50
MBSR (mindfulness based stress reduction) 50, 59
McCaw, C. T. 21
McGhee, P. 41, 43
McLean, G. N. 59
McMindfulness 20–21
meditation 15, 45, 50, 72, 75–76, 116, 119, 124; body part contemplation 15–16; body scan 15, 87, 88–89, 124, 126; breath work 15, 16, 87–88, 116, 119, 124, 126; chocolate 91–92; (emotional) self-awareness 106–107; empty 94; prospection of desire and purpose 112–113; quiet your mind 95–96; smile 91, 92–93; Sutra 97, 98–99; teacher training courses 50, 51; walking 48, 49
mEDucation unlocked podcast 64
Medvedev, O. 62
Melissen, F. 21
mental states 17–18
Mielke, F. 9
mind: contracted (constricted) 94; distortion of 105; distracted 44, 46, 94–95; mindfulness of 13–14, 17–18, 30, 86, 93–96, 136, 139–141, 143
Mind and Life Education Research Network 133
mind—body dichotomy 35
Mindful Attention Awareness Scale (MAAS) 45, 46
mindful reflexivity 43, 133
mindfulness: as a choice 3–4; commercial exploitation of 20–21; conceptual research 26; definitions of 13; empirical research 26; foundations of *see* foundations of mindfulness; as personality trait 8–9; and religion/spiritual traditions 8, *see also* Buddha/Buddhism; as state of mind 8–9; thin and thick 21; as a word 9
mindfulness *as* education 26, 27–28

mindfulness based cognitive therapy (MBCT) 50
mindfulness based stress reduction (MBSR) 50, 59
mindfulness and business education 9, 26, 28; educational concepts for 52–54; facilitation 48–52; measuring effectiveness in the classroom 46–48; purpose of 42–46
mindfulness coaching 80–81, 99, 116–130; for business educators 126–129; coaching questions 96–8, 106, 107, 116; intention setting 89, 119; peer to peer 123–126; and personal tutoring 120–122; SMART framework 119; tools 125–126
mindfulness *in* education 26–27
mindfulness language, adoption of 134–135
mindfulness *of* education 26, 28
mindfulness relationship 11–13
mindfulness teaching *see* teaching mindfulness
mission statements 134–135, 136, 137
Mitchell, C. 112
mobile devices, as distractions 46
module level integration 84, 102–115
mood meters 45
Moore, Z. E. 9
moral intelligence 53–54
moral responsibility 133
morality 20
Moratis, L. 21
Mortari, L. 53
motivation 44, 73, 97, 104; intrinsic 113, 114
multiple intelligences 64
musical intelligence 64

Nanus, B. 29
Nason, R. 30
Nathan, M. J. 35
naturalistic intelligence 64
Neale, M. 21
neo-liberalism 20, 26
Nesbit, P. 111
Nestor, J. 89
nonself 43
Norré, B. F. 42, 43, 45, 49
Northouse, P. G. 47
Nyland, C. 25

O'Brien, J. 103
observing 29
Oettingen, G. 112
Ollie (case example) 10–11
Omar, A. 102
online mindfulness training 7

open-ended questions 117, 125
openness: approaching uncertainty with 133; cultivation of 43, 54
Osiemo, L. B. 131
O'Toole, J. 26

Page, M. L. 104–105
Panchal, S. 116
Pandya, B. 62
Parilla, E. S. 132, 136, 142
Passmore, J. 118
pausing 29
Peck, S. C. 133
pedagogy: of care/self-care 52–53, 54; contemplative 52, 54; for humanised leadership 52, 53–54
peer coaching 117, 123–126
perception: distortion of 105; embodied 35
Perrakis, A. 75
person-oriented coaching 117, 118, 127
personal and professional development 50, 52, 71, 84–85, 102, 117
personal tutoring 120–122; SEEC (supporting, empowering, enhancing, connecting) model 120–121; TUNE (Trust – Us – Needs – Evaluate) framework 121
personality 8–9
Petchsawang, P. 59
Plaskoff, J. 33
playfulness 79–80
popular culture mindfulness books 9
postgraduate programmes 84–85, 102; *see also* MBA students
Postlewaite, A. 116
practical wisdom 34
presence 46; learning by 33; physical 44
privilege 61
professional development *see* personal and professional development
programme/course level integration 84–101; case study *see* 'Enrich Your Study Life' case study; consideration 99–100; credit-bearing modules 84; personal and professional development streams 84–85
proprioception 35
prospection 112–113
purpose: business schools 136–137; identifying 112–113
purpose of mindfulness and business education 42–46; encouraging openness and ethical decision making 42–44; enhancing emotional intelligence 44–46
Purser, R. 20–21, 28, 60

qualification in mindfulness 50–51
questioning 117, 119, 125
quiet your mind meditation 95–96

rationality 43
Reb, J. 9, 141
receptiveness 53
reflection/self-reflection 53, 61, 111–112, 119, 124–125, 125–126
reflective podcasts 84
reflexivity, mindful 43, 133
Reid, A. 117, 127
Reina, C. S. 9
relational leadership 35
relationship management 106
religions 8; *see also* Buddha/Buddhism
remembering (*Sati*) 13
resilience 42, 54, 85, 103, 104, 114, 134, 139
respect 22
responsibility 22, 33, 54, 131–132, 133; moral 133
responsiveness 53
restlessness 18, 19, 96, 142
Review of Education 26
Reynolds, M. 43
Riddell, P. 116
risk assessment 52
Rivers, C. 44, 62, 64, 103
Robbins, C. R. 35
Roberts, C. 41
Robertson, L. 44
Roche, M. 85
Roeser, R. W. 133
Rosen, L. D. 44
Rosenboom, A. 62
Roy, A. 80
Rubens, A. 102
Rust, R. T. 63
Ryan, R. M. 9, 46, 47

Sadler-Smith, E. 41, 43, 48, 49, 85
safeguarding 53
Sánchez-Flores, M. J. 61
Santorelli, S. F. 33
Sati (remembering) 13
satipatthana see foundations of mindfulness
Sauer, S. 104
Saunders, P. A. 111
Scharmer, O. 135
Schultz, P. P. 47
scientific–based mindfulness research 9
SEEC (supporting, empowering, enhancing, connecting) model 120–121
self-acceptance 76, 93–96

self-actualisation 33, 129
self-awareness 33, 47, 52, 90–93, 103, 106–108, 110, 114; artificial intelligence (AI) and 63, 65; assessment 110; business education strategy and 132; conceptual 35; DEI and 61; embodied 35, 36; emotional 106–107; emotional intelligence and 44, 45–46, 54; insights and actions for development of 108; internal and external 35–36, 47, 59, 90, 93, 123–124, 125, 126; mindfulness coaching and 118, 123–126; recall 107; reflection and prospection and development of 111; sharing circle 108
self-belief 76
self-care 52–53, 103, 108–109; case study: Managing self-care at work 109
self-compassion 76, 138
self-doubt 116
self-knowledge 49, 111, 124
self-management 106
self-practice 49–50
self-reflection 53, 61
self-regulation 44
sense spheres, internal and external 19, 35
Seppälä, E. 85
Seraj, S. 122, 125
service aspects of business education strategy 140
Sezer, O. 42
Sharma, R. 8, 19
Shefy, E. 42, 43, 48, 49, 85
Shelly, R. 118
should narrative 78–79
silence, being comfortable with 117
Sims, D. 34
skills development: leadership 32–33; teaching mindfulness 48–49
Skinner, B. F. 73
sleep 109
Sliwa, M. 34
sloth 18–19, 94, 96, 142
Slutsky, J. 58
Small, C. 133
SMART framework 119
smile meditation 91, 92–93
Smith, A. 119, 125
Smolansky, A. 62
Snook, S. 136
social awareness 106
social and residential success 104
social skills 44
Socrates 52
somatic intelligence 35, 36, 63

Spender, J. C. 25
Spinelli, C. 133
spiritual intelligence 53–54
spiritual traditions 8
spirituality 59
Spronken-Smith, R. 104
Stedham, Y. 42, 43
strategy *see* business education strategy
stress 17, 18, 27, 42, 47, 48, 58–59, 118
student engagement 44, 46; academic engagement 104; in extracurricular activities 71–72, 73
student performance, mindfulness and 46–47
success 103–105; concept map 105; definitions of 104; performance measures 104; visual inquiry-based research 104–105
suffering 8, 18–19, 63, 141, 142; liberation from 28; noble truths about 19–20
Sumell, A. J. 42, 46
sun salutations 77
sustainability 53, 59–60, 65, 133
Sustainable Development Goals (SDGs) 60
Sutra coaching questions 97–8
Sutra meditation 97, 98–99
System 1 and System 2 thinking 42

Tao Te Ching (Tzu) 100, 114, 129, 143
Taylor, E. 139
Taylor, V. F. 45–46
teaching mindfulness 48–52; codes of conduct and ethics 51; and experiential pedagogy 51–52; and professional development 50, 51; qualifications 50–51; and self-practice 49–50; skills development 48–49
technology 65; distractions by 44, 46
thin and thick mindfulness 21
thinking fast and thinking slow 42
Thomas, W. 119, 125
Thomason, S. J. 117
Tolle, E. 139
torpor 18–19, 94, 142
Town, S. 41
tree yoga pose 77–78, *78*
triple bottom line 21
trust 53, 121
truthful path 18, 19
TUNE (Trust – Us – Needs – Evaluate) framework 121
Tzu, L., *Tao Te Ching* 100, 114, 129, 143

uncertainty 28, 29–30, 133

United Nations Principles of Responsible Management Education (UN PRME) 60
United Nations Sustainable Development Goals (SDGs) 60
Usprech, J. 108
Uysal, M. 63

van Den Assem, B. 118
Van Fleet, D. D. 24
Verducci, S. 116
Vince, R. 43
vision 29, 134, 136, 137
visual intelligence 64
visualisation 15, 45
volatility 28, 29
Vu, M. C. 42
VUCA frameworks 28–30, 42

Walker, R. 104
walking meditation 48, 49
Walton, I. 34
Wamsler, C. 59, 60
Wang, Y.–C. 63
Warrior Three yoga pose 78–79, *79*
Waterman Jr, R. H. 132
Weger Jr, H. 117
wellbeing 9, 21, 26, 41, 46, 47, 60, 82, 102, 104, 108, 109, 110, 118, 120, 138; employee 58–59, 65
Wharton's School of Finance and Economy 24
wheel of conditioned existence (Wheel of Samsāra)) 19
wisdom 20, 27, 62; bodily 35; practical 34
Wolever, R. Q. 58, 59
Wolfenden, S. 89
work—life balance/conflicts 58–59, 108
World Economic Forum 59–60
worry 18, 19, 63, 80–81, 86–87, 96, 142
Wren, D. A. 24

Yanovska, V. 117
yoga 15, 47, 50, 72, 76–80, 116; sun salutations 77; teacher training courses 50; tree pose 77–78, *78*; Warrior Three pose 78–79, *79*
yogastah kuru karmani mantra 112–113
Young, T. 47

Zaidman, N. 118
Zanjonc, A. 52
Zbierowski, P. 59
Zeff, S. A. 25
Zivnuska, S. 58
Zu, L. 135

Printed in the United States
by Baker & Taylor Publisher Services